COLLI

CW00672825

EDINBURGH
STREETFINDER
ATLAS

CONTENTS

HarperCollins*Publishers*

Collins Edinburgh Streetfinder Atlas

Collins
An Imprint of HarperCollins*Publishers*
77-85 Fulham Palace Road, Hammersmith, London W6 8JB

Copyright © HarperCollins*Publishers* Ltd 1998

Maps © Bartholomew Ltd 1992, 1995, 1997

Based upon the Ordnance Survey mapping with the permission of the Controller of Her Majesty's Stationery Office. © Crown copyright 399302.

Printed in Hong Kong

ISBN 0 00 448714 1   LNR   LI9659

Legend

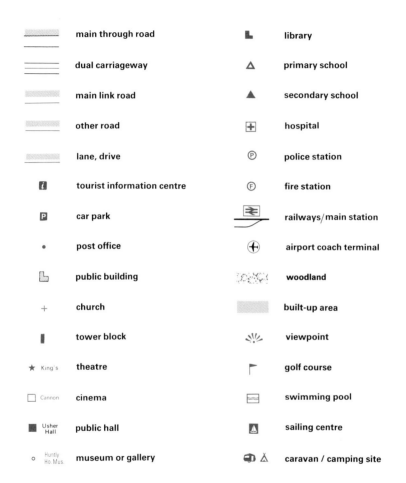

	main through road		**L**	library
	dual carriageway		△	primary school
	main link road		▲	secondary school
	other road		⊞	hospital
	lane, drive		℗	police station
i	tourist information centre		Ⓕ	fire station
P	car park		⇄	railways/main station
•	post office		⊕	airport coach terminal
⌐	public building			woodland
+	church			built-up area
▮	tower block		☀	viewpoint
★ King's	theatre		⌐	golf course
□ Cannon	cinema		⊟	swimming pool
■ Usher Hall	public hall		⚠	sailing centre
○ Huntly Ho.Mus.	museum or gallery		🚐 Å	caravan / camping site

Scale of main map pages - 1:15 000 (4.2 inches to 1 mile)

0	0.5	1	1.5 km
0	¼	½	¾ 1 mile

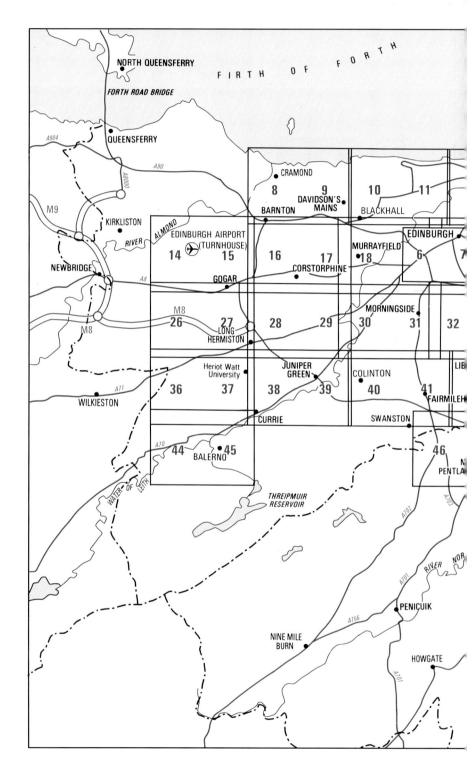

NORTH QUEENSFERRY

FORTH ROAD BRIDGE

FIRTH OF FORTH

A904

QUEENSFERRY

A90

A8000

M9

KIRKLISTON

RIVER ALMOND

EDINBURGH AIRPORT
(TURNHOUSE)

CRAMOND

8 9
DAVIDSON'S
MAINS

BARNTON

10 11

BLACKHALL

EDINBURGH

NEWBRIDGE

14 15

GOGAR

16 17
CORSTORPHINE

MURRAYFIELD
18

6 7

A8

M8

26 27
LONG
HERMISTON

28 29

30

MORNINGSIDE

31 32

M8

Heriot Watt
University

JUNIPER
GREEN

COLINTON

LIB

WILKIESTON

A71

36 37

38 39

40

41
FAIRMILEH

CURRIE

SWANSTON

A70

44 45
BALERNO

46
N
PENTLA

WATER OF LEITH

THREIPMUIR
RESERVOIR

A702

A703

RIVER NOR

A701

A766

PENICUIK

NINE MILE
BURN

A701

HOWGATE

KEY TO MAP PAGES

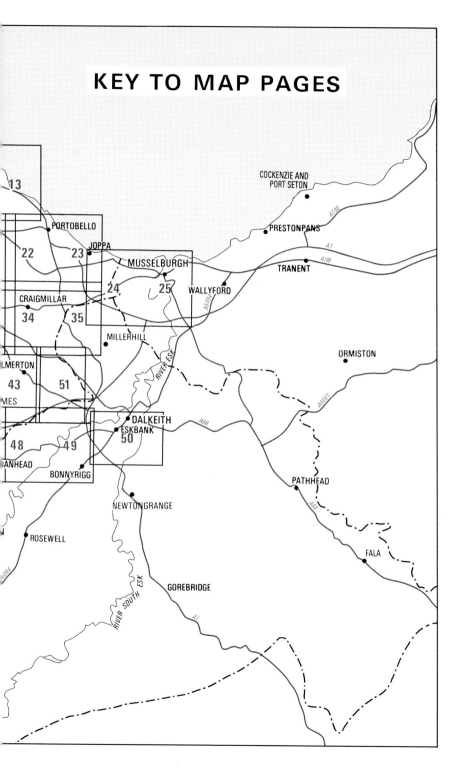

COCKENZIE AND
PORT SETON

13

PORTOBELLO

PRESTONPANS

JOPPA

22   23

MUSSELBURGH

TRANENT

24   25   WALLYFORD

CRAIGMILLAR

34   35

MILLERHILL

ORMISTON

LMERTON

43   51

RIVER ESK

MES

DALKEITH

ESKBANK

48   49   50

ANHEAD

BONNYRIGG

PATHHEAD

NEWTONGRANGE

ROSEWELL

FALA

GOREBRIDGE

RIVER SOUTH ESK

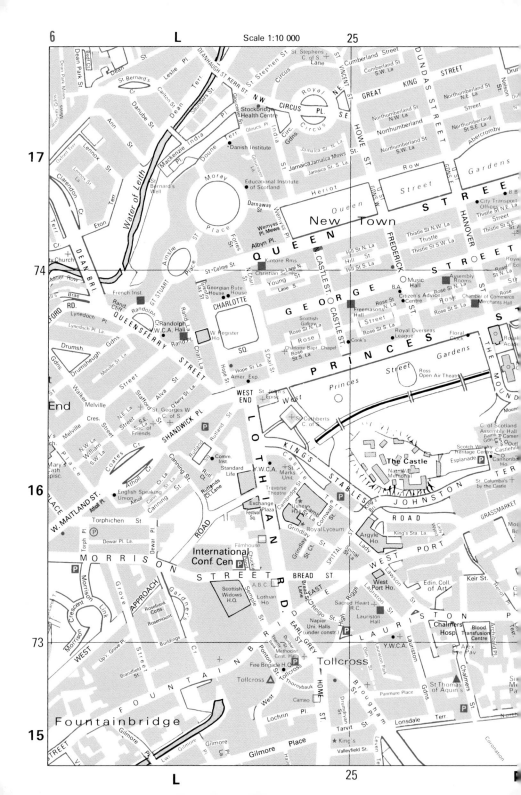

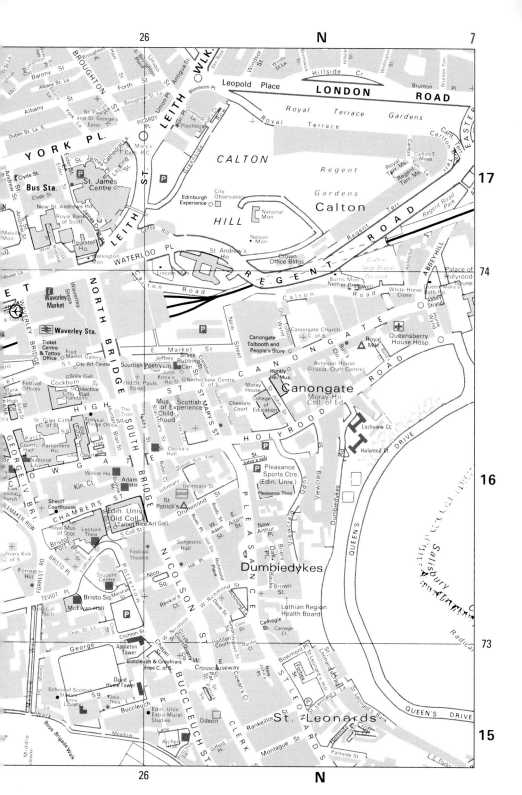

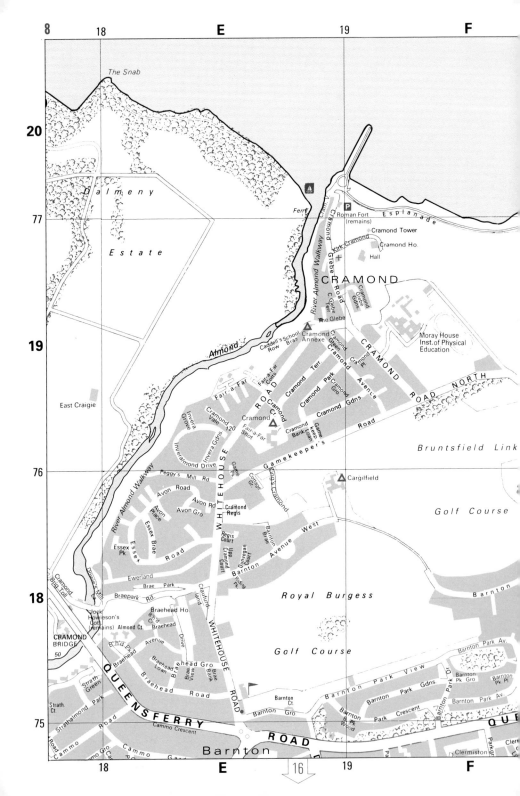

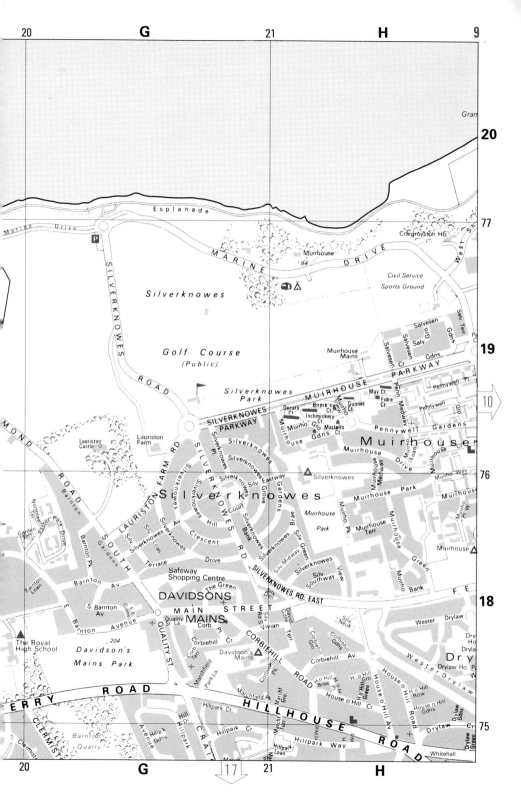

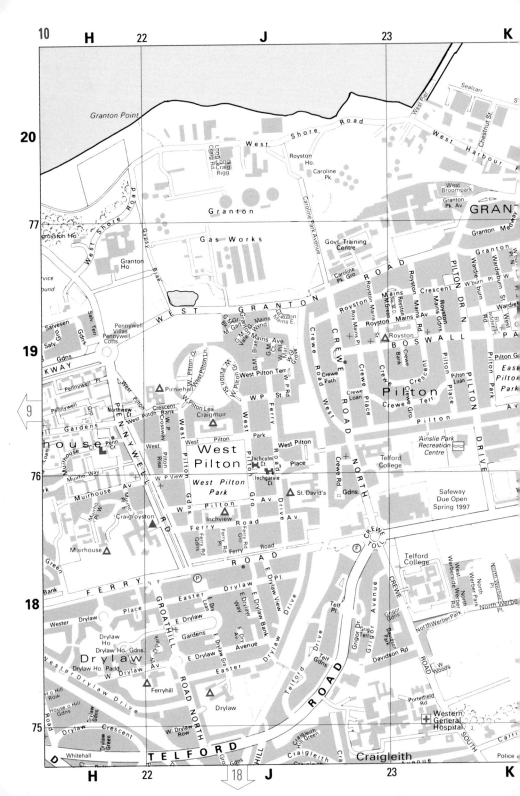

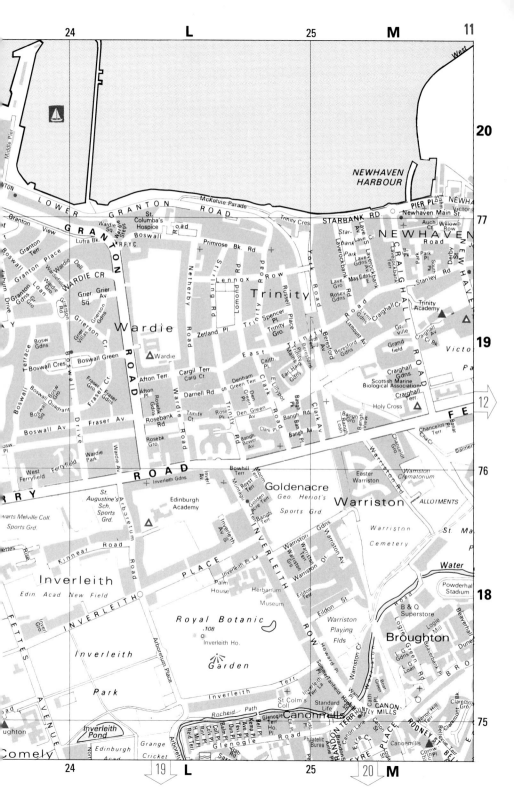

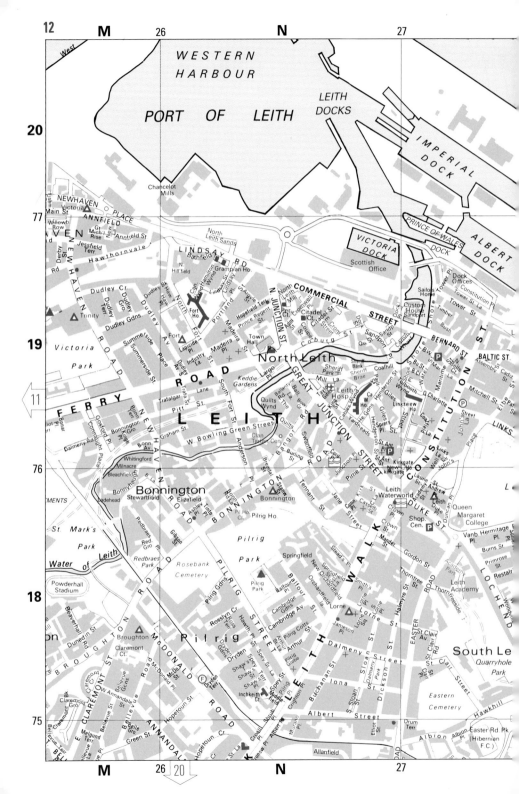

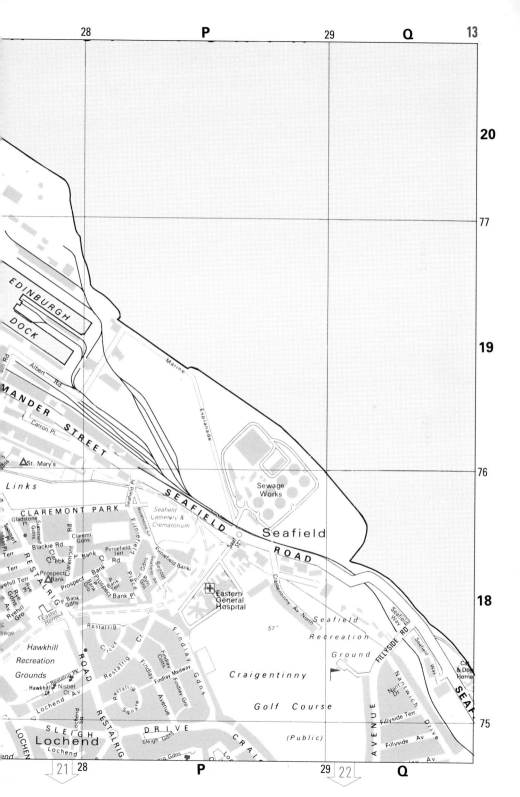

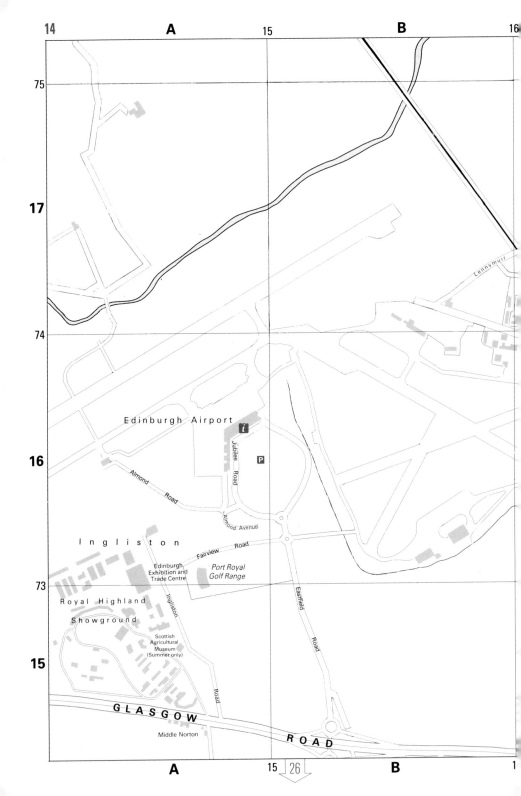

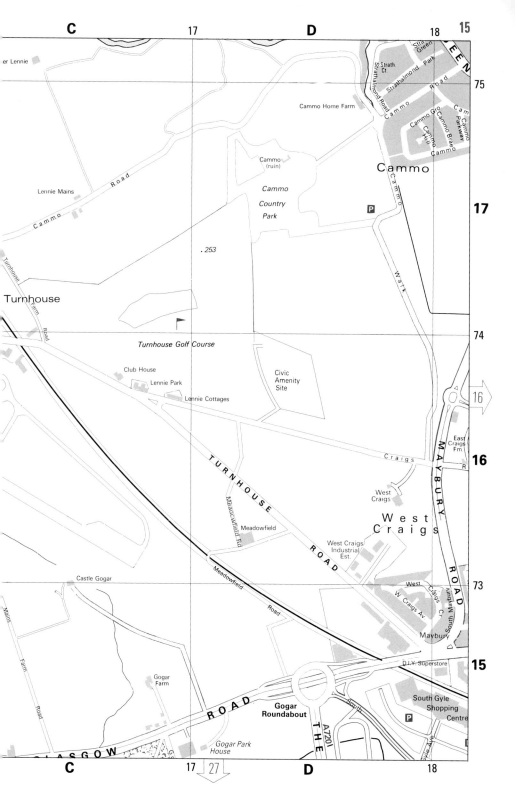

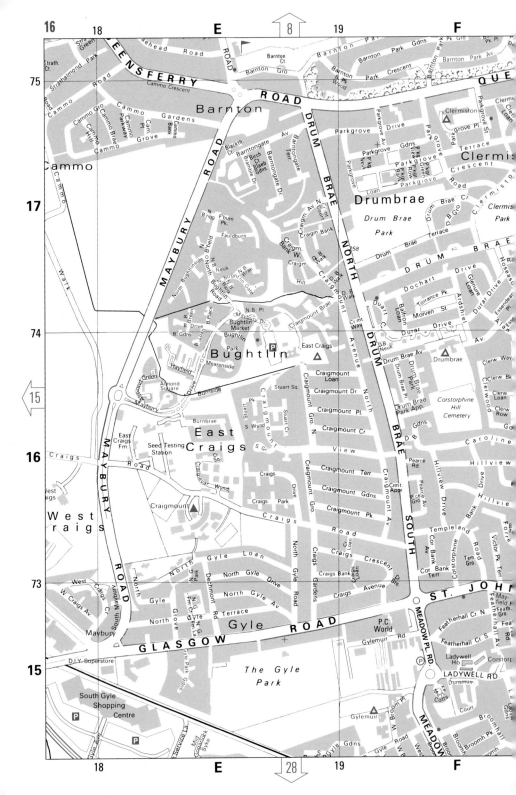

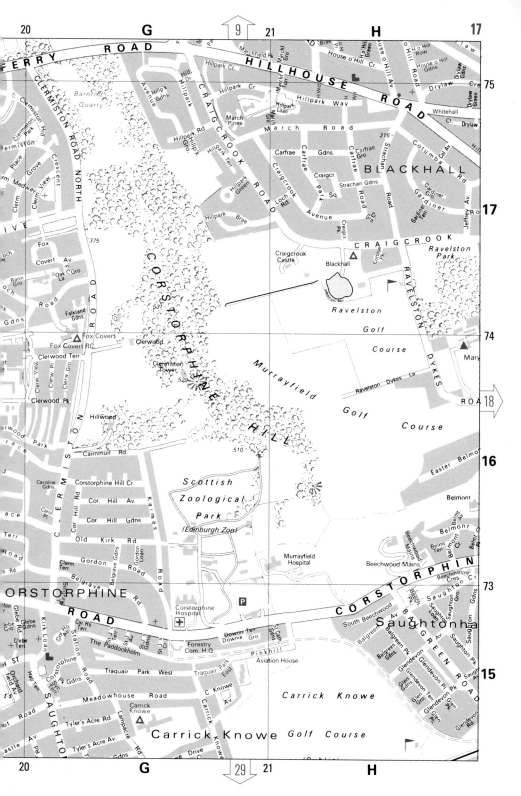

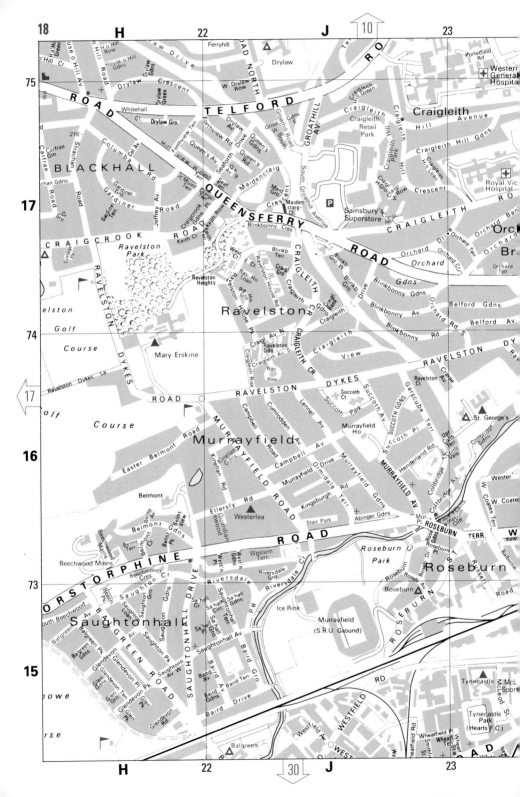

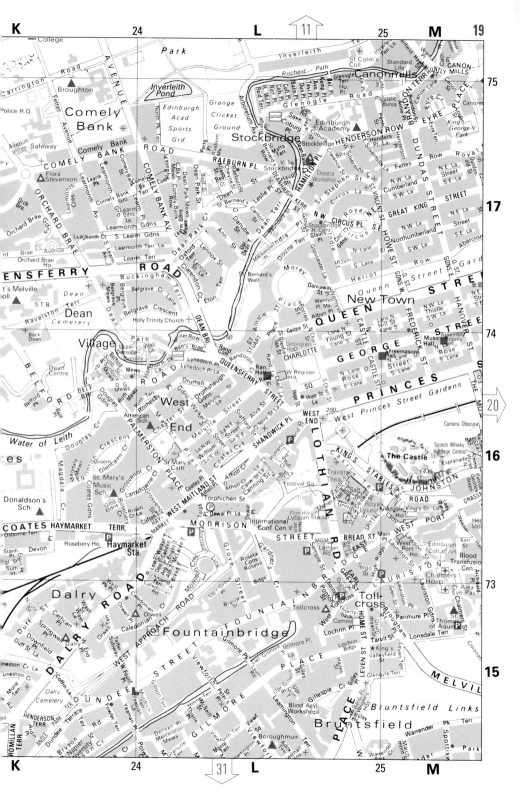

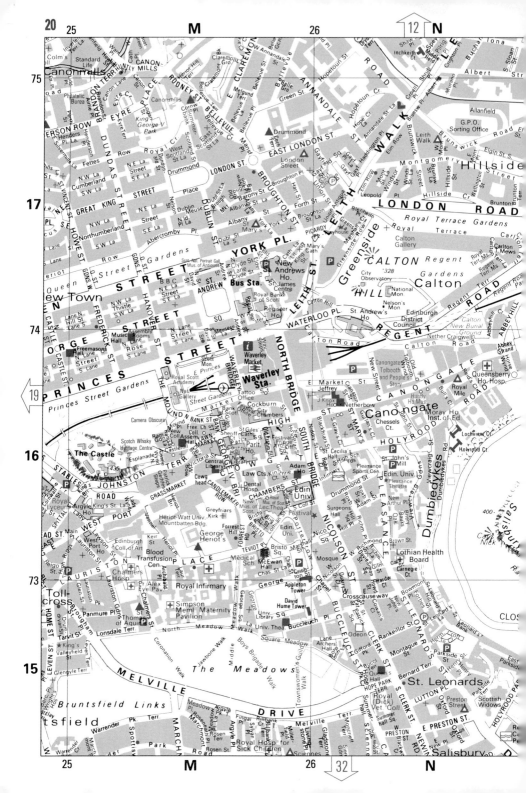

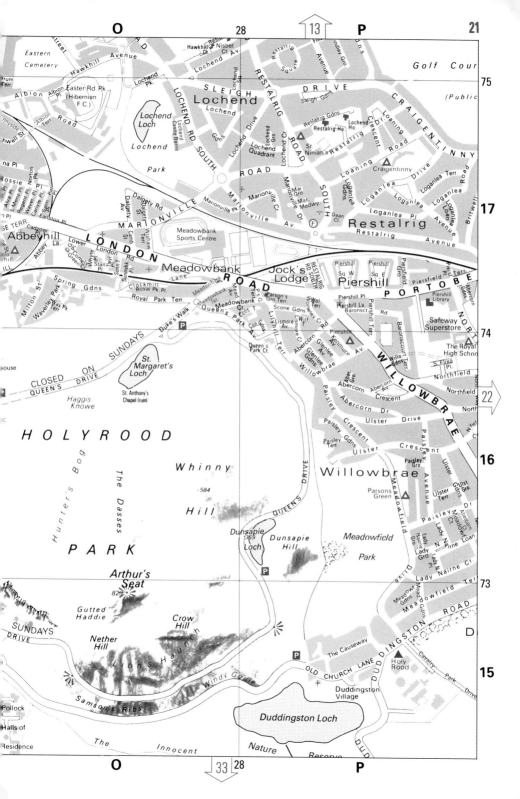

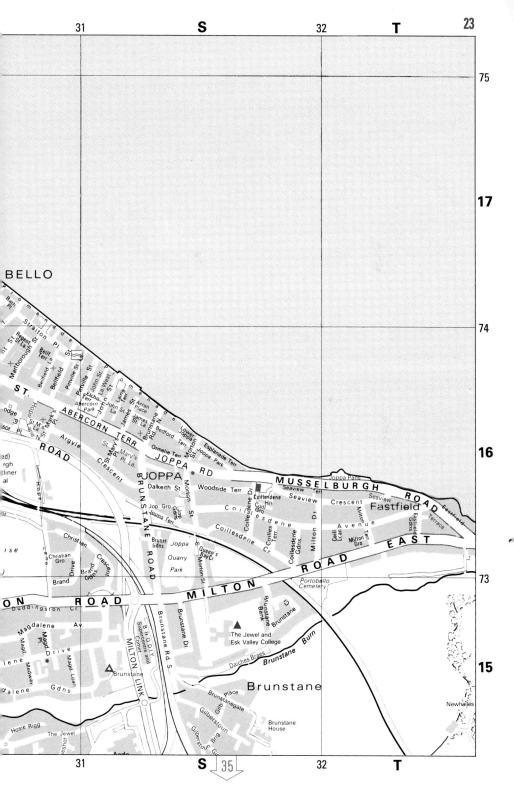

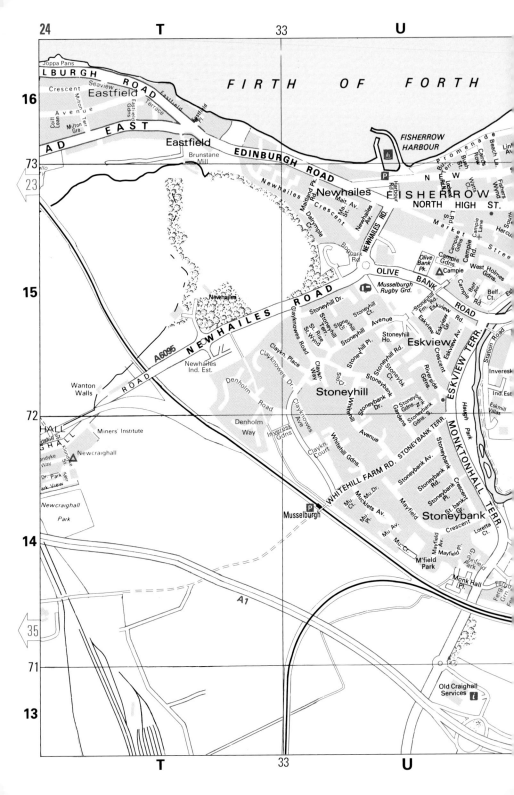

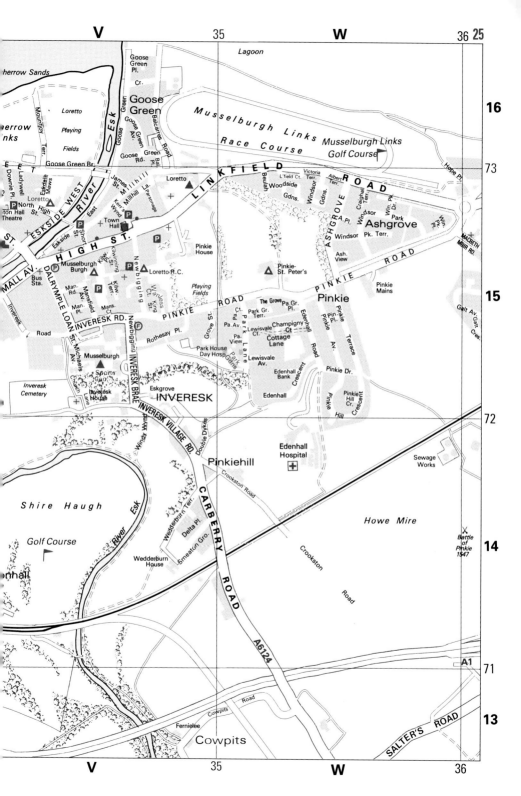

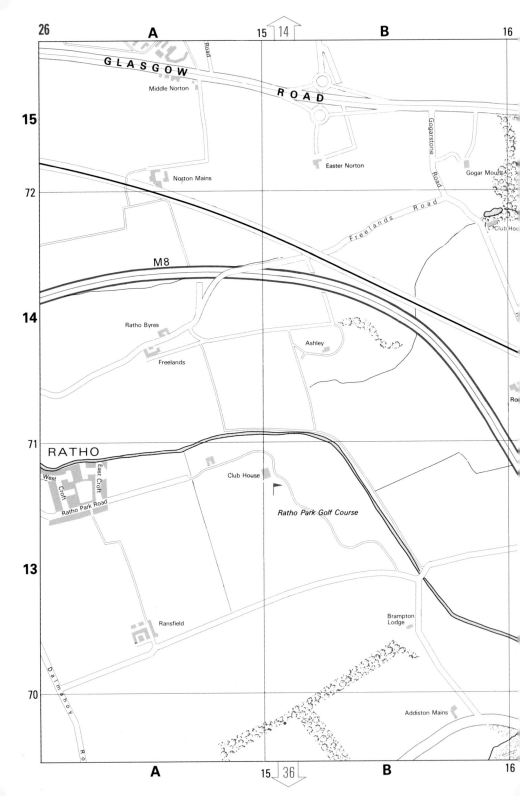

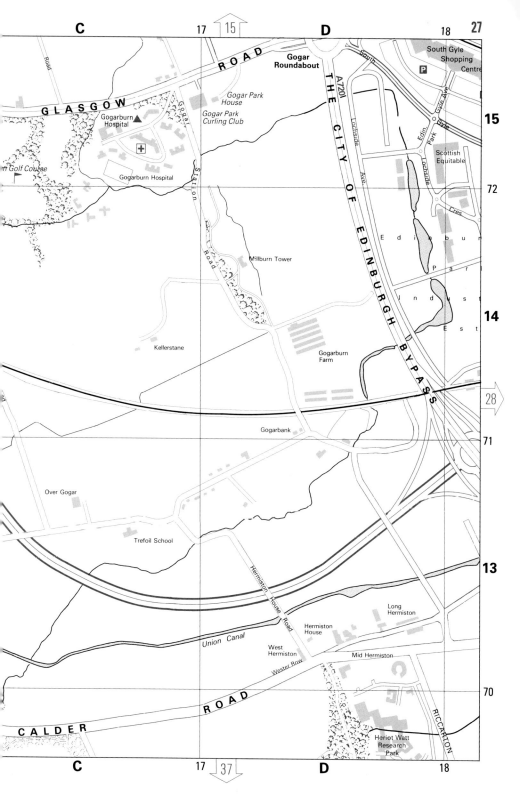

GLASGOW ROAD

Gogar Roundabout

Gogar Park House

Gogar Park Curling Club

Gogar Park

Gogarburn Hospital

Gogarburn Hospital

Road

n Golf Course

Gogar

Station Road

A720

THE CITY OF EDINBURGH BYPASS

South

Lochside Ave.

Lochside

Lochside

Edin

Gyle Park Ave.

GYLE

South Gyle Shopping Centre

P

Scottish Equitable

Edin

bur

Cres

Par

n

du s

Es t

15

72

14

Millburn Tower

Kellerstane

Gogarburn Farm

Gogarbank

28

71

Over Gogar

Trefoil School

Hermiston House Road

13

Long Hermiston

Hermiston House

Union Canal

West Hermiston

Mid Hermiston

Wester Row

70

CALDER ROAD

RICCARTON

Heriot Watt Research Park

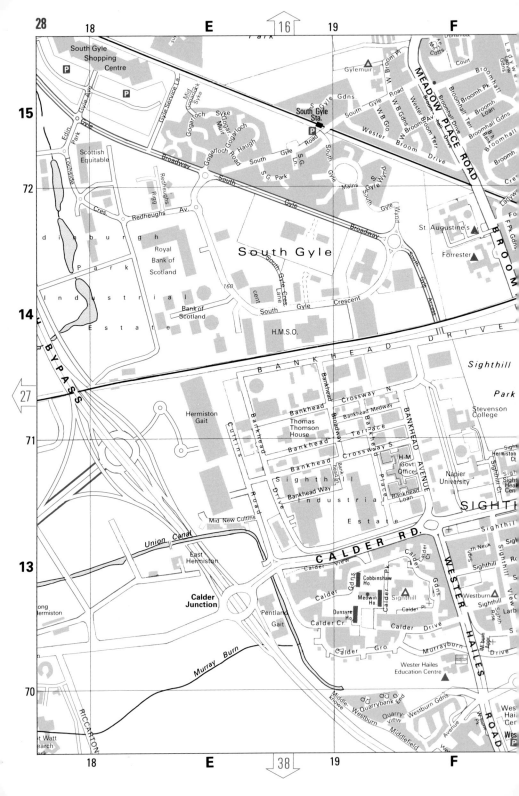

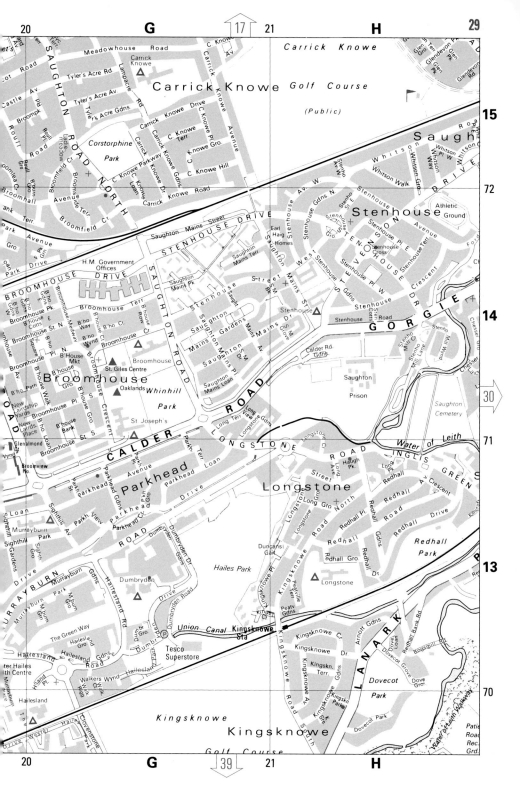

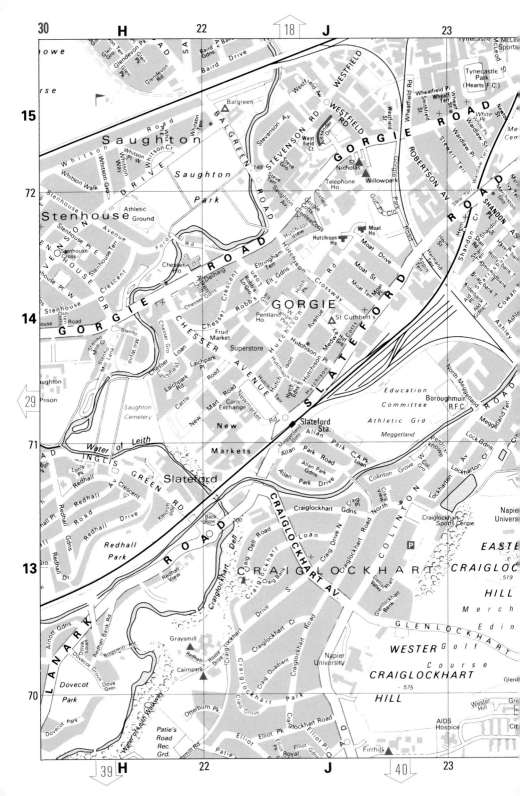

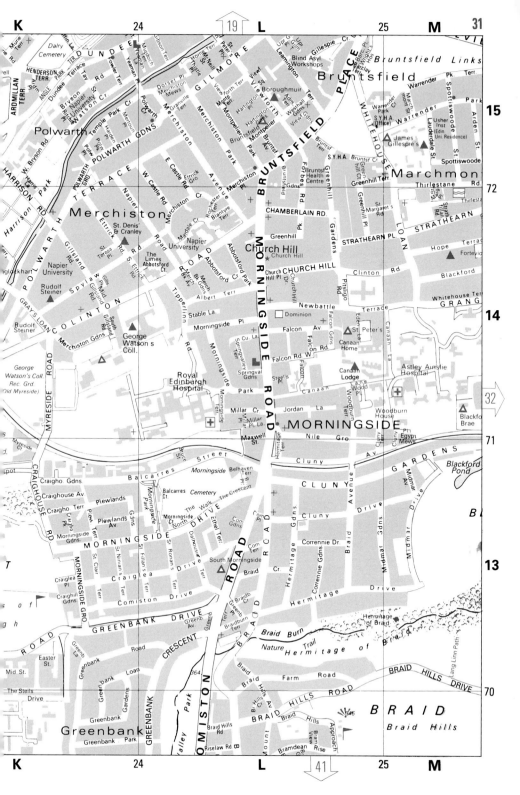

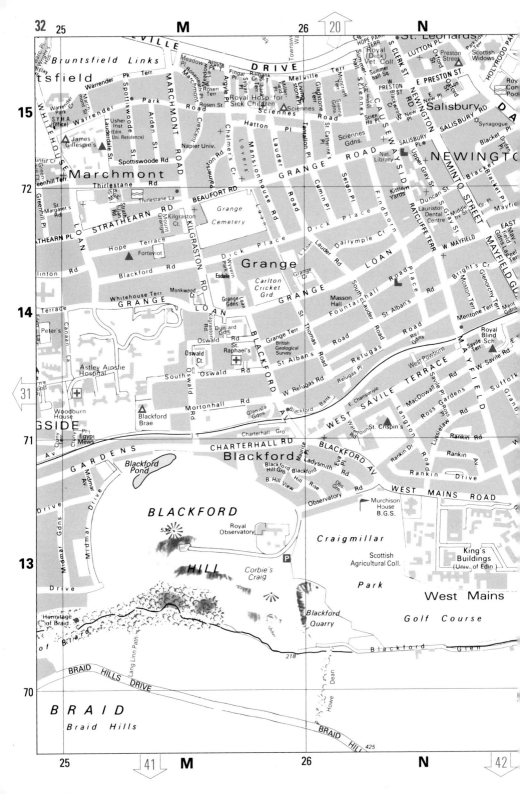

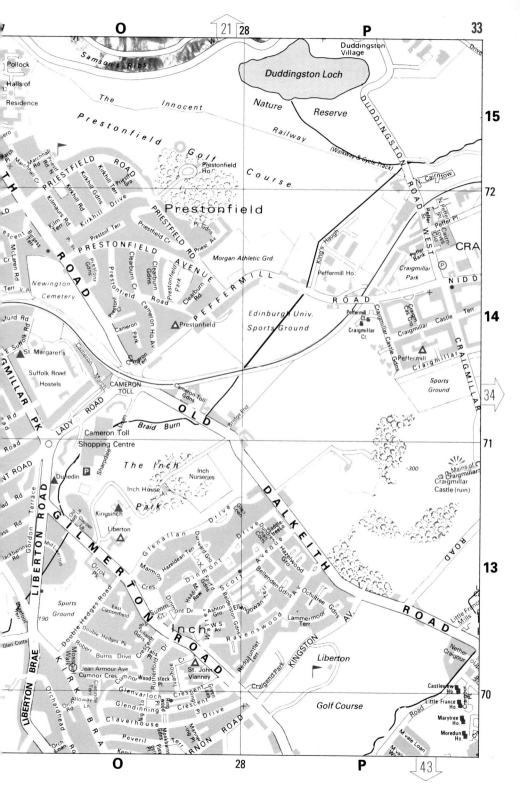

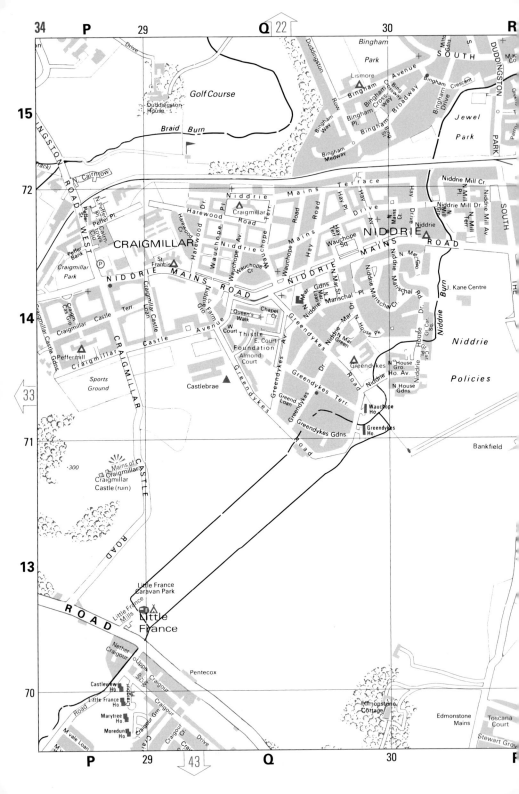

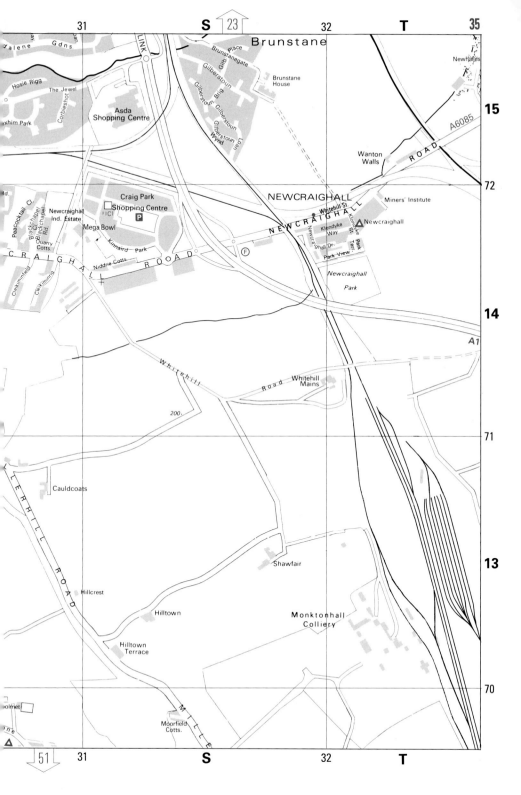

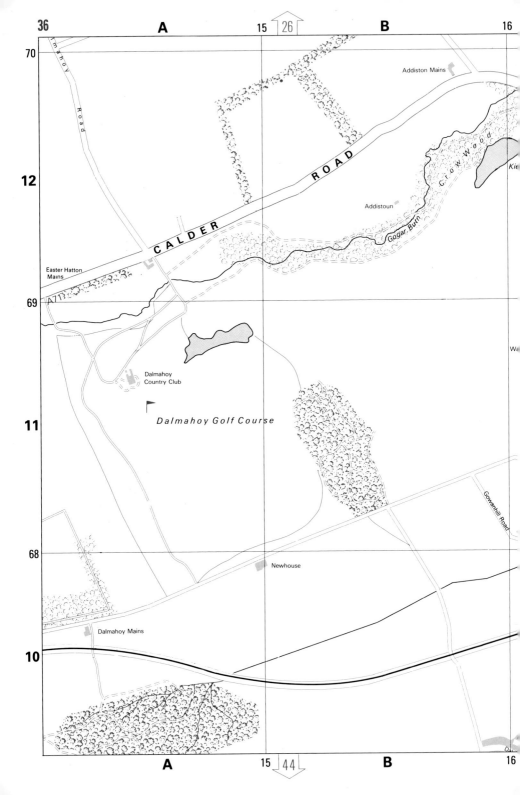

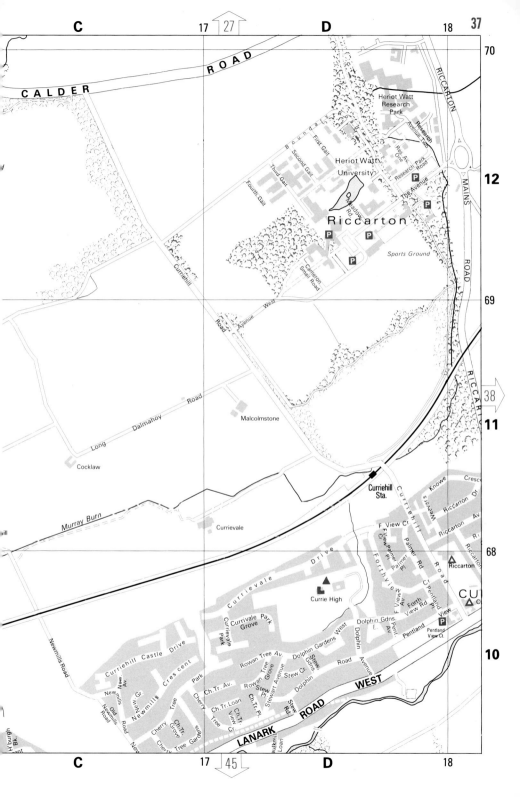

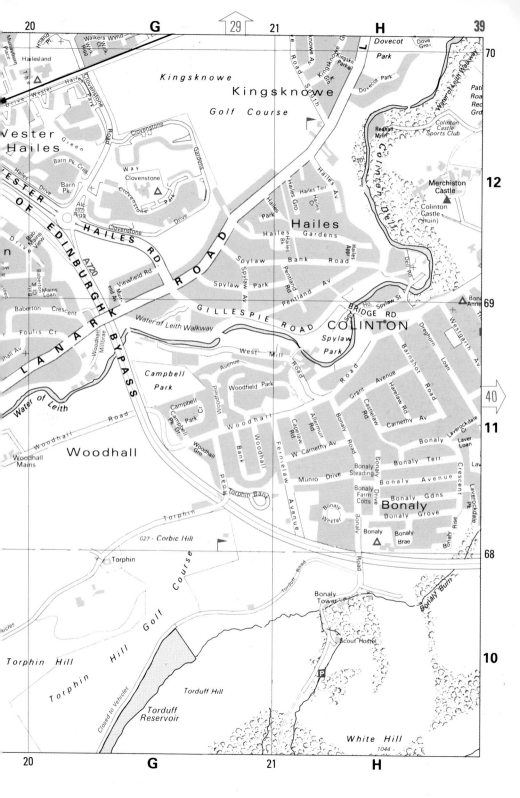

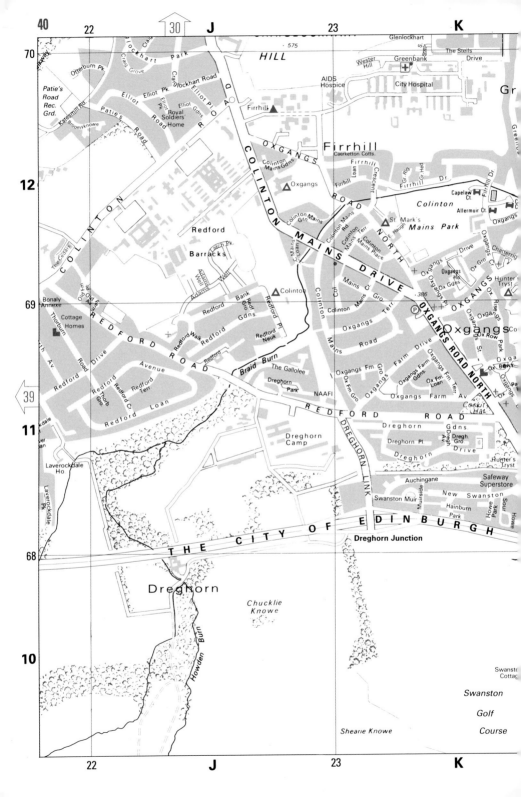

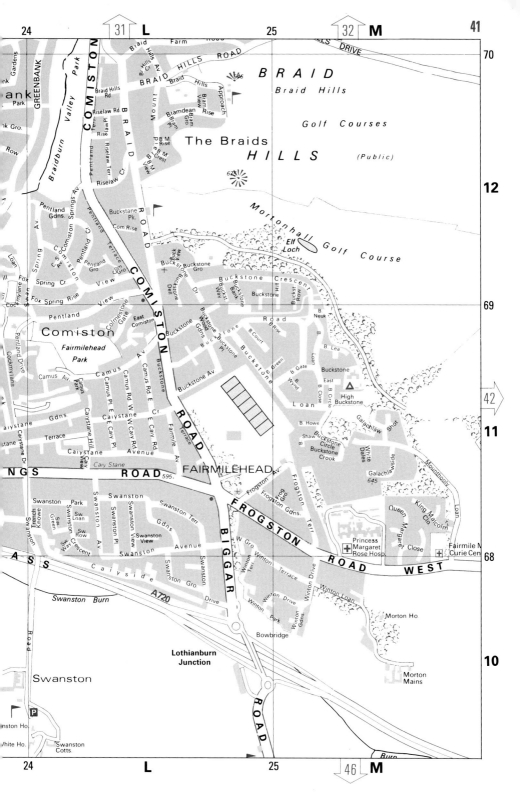

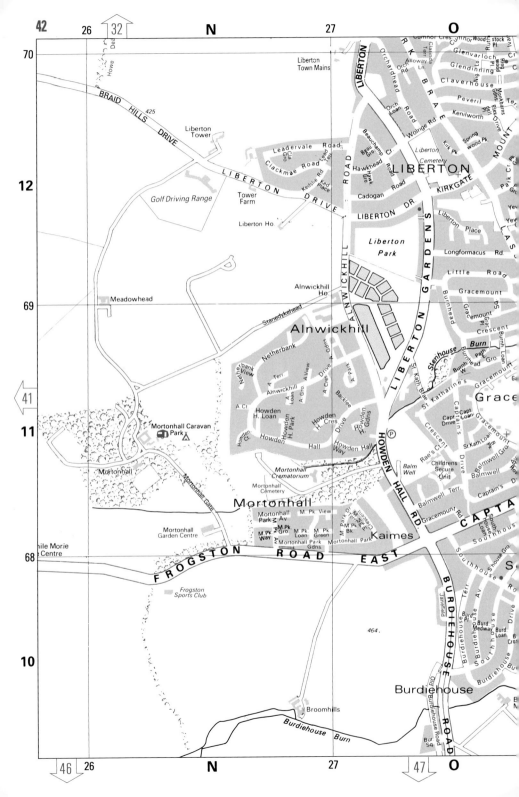

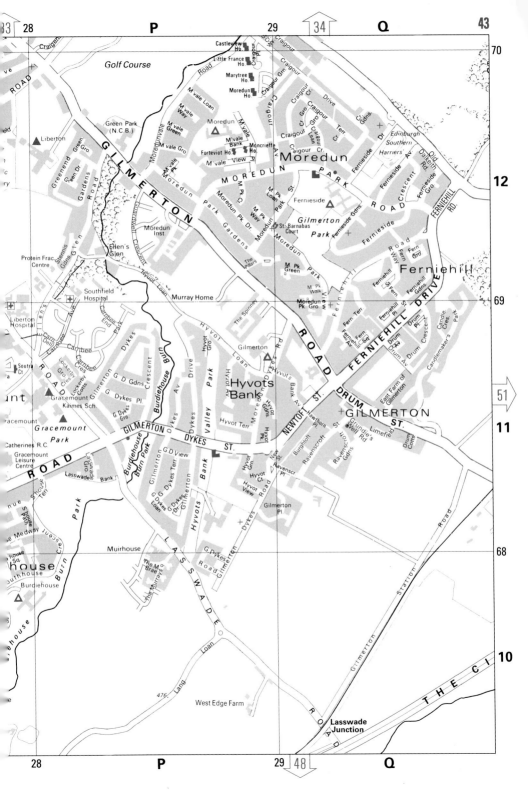

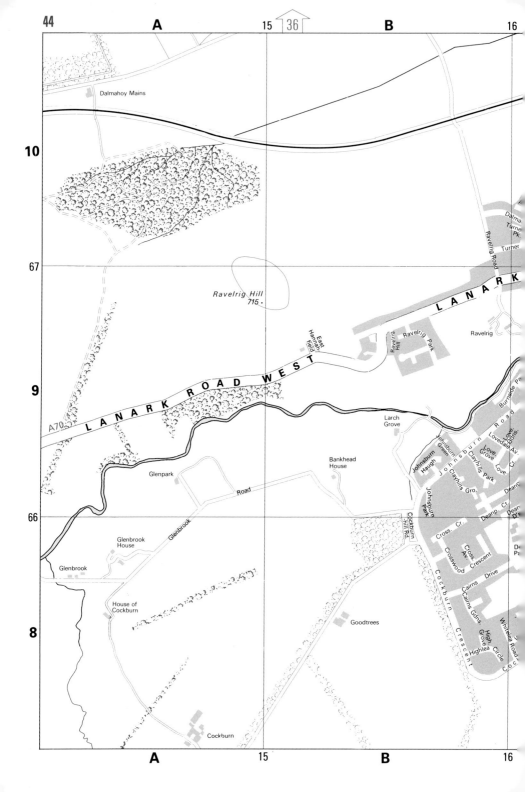

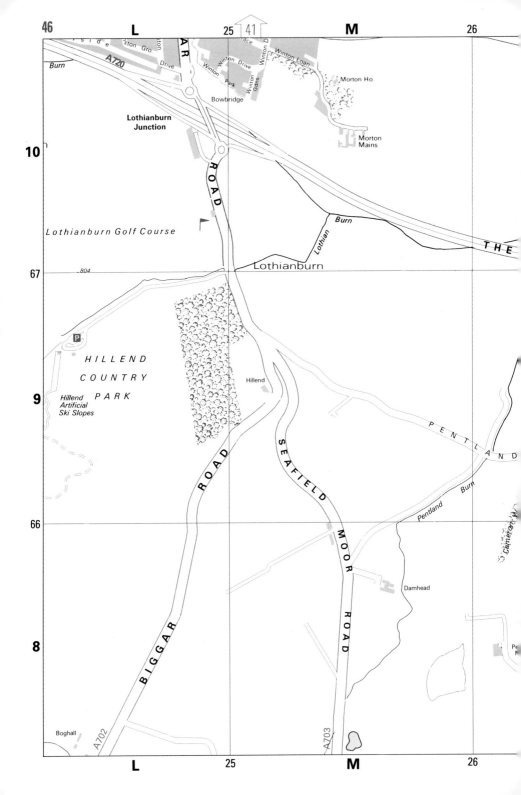

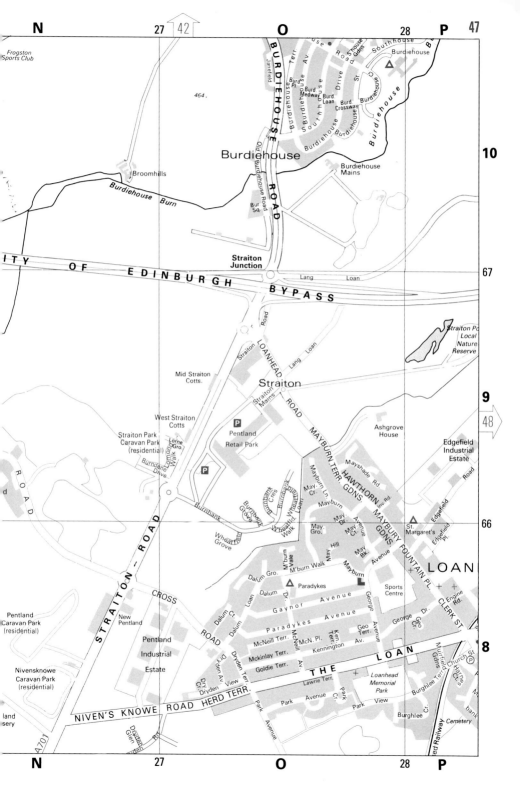

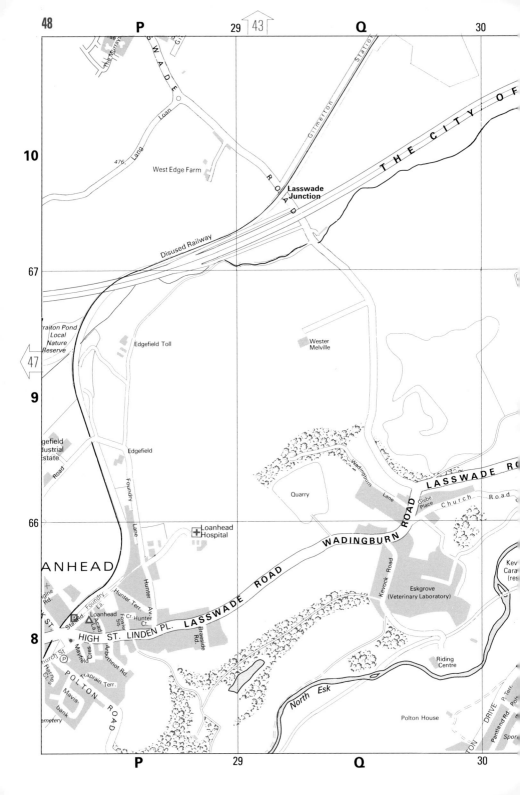

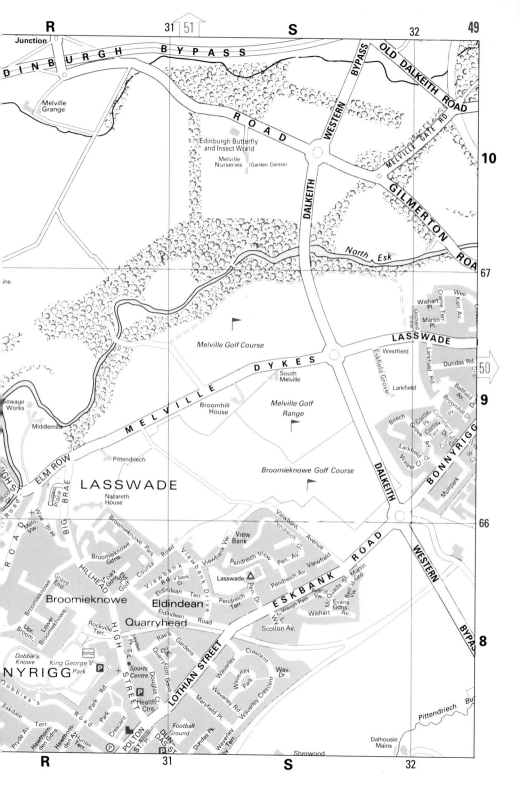

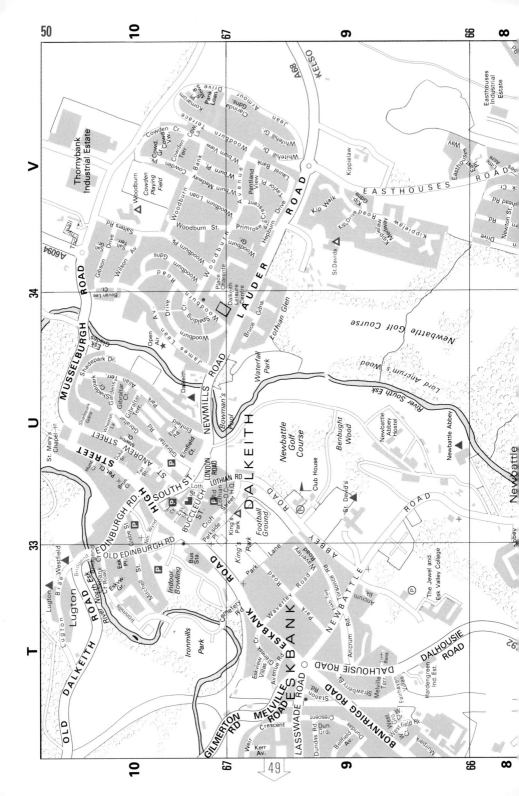

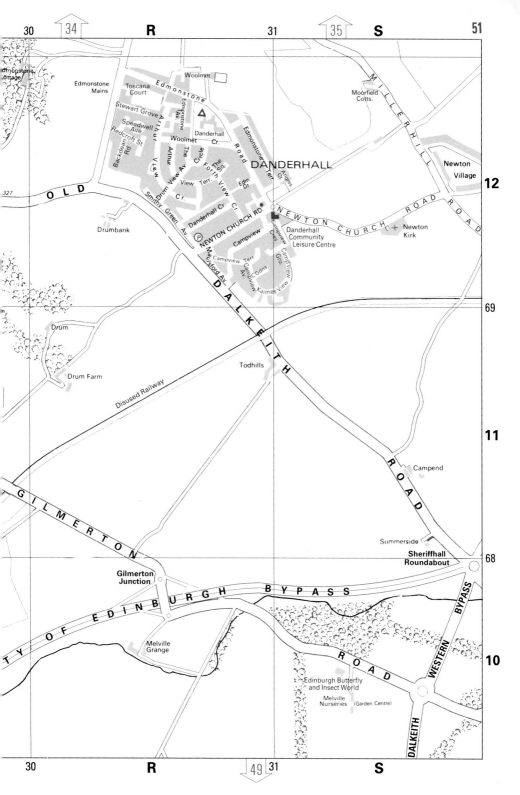

INDEX TO STREETS

General Abbreviations

Acad.	Academy	Ct.	Court	Ho.	House	R.F.C.	Rugby Football Club
All.	Alley	Cts.	Courts	Hos.	Houses	Rd.	Road
App.	Approach	Dr.	Drive	Hosp.	Hospital	Ri.	Rise
Arc.	Arcade	E.	East	Ind.	Industrial	S.	South
Av.	Avenue	Esp.	Esplanade	Junct.	Junction	Sch.	School
Bdy.	Broadway	Est.	Estate	La.	Lane	Sq.	Square
Bk.	Bank	Ex.	Exchange	Ln.	Loan	St.	Street, Saint
Bldgs.	Buildings	Fld.	Field	Lo.	Lodge	Sta.	Station
Bri.	Bridge	Flds.	Fields	Lwr.	Lower	Ter.	Terrace
Cem.	Cemetery	Fm.	Farm	Mem.	Memorial	Twr.	Tower
Cen.	Centre	G.P.O.	General Post Office	Mkt.	Market	Vills.	Villas
Cft.	Croft	Gall.	Gallery	Ms.	Mews	Vw.	View
Ch.	Church	Gdn.	Garden	Mt.	Mount	W.	West
Circ.	Circle	Gdns.	Gardens	N.	North	Wd.	Wood
Clo.	Close	Gra.	Grange	Par.	Parade	Wds.	Woods
Coll.	College	Grd.	Ground	Pk.	Park	Wf.	Wharf
Cor.	Corner	Grn.	Green	Pl.	Place	Wr.	Wester
Cotts.	Cottages	Grns.	Greens	Pt.	Port	Yd.	Yard
Crem.	Crematorium	Gro.	Grove	Quad.	Quadrant		
Cres.	Crescent	H.Q.	Head Quarters	R.C.	Roman Catholic		

Post Town Abbreviations

NB. All entries are for Edinburgh Post Town unless otherwise stated.

Bal.	Balerno	Jun.Grn.	Juniper Green	Muss.	Musselburgh
Bonny.	Bonnyrigg	Lass.	Lasswade	Newbr.	Newbridge
Dalk.	Dalkeith	Loanh.	Loanhead		

District Abbreviations

Cram.	Cramond	Inglis.	Ingliston	Ricc.	Riccarton
Dand.	Danderhall	Inver.	Inveresk	Strait.	Straiton
David.	Davidsons Mains	Monk.	Monktonhall	White.	Whitecraig
Easth.	Easthouses	Newcr.	Newcraighall	Wool.	Woolmet

Name		
Buckstane Pk. EH10	41	L12
Buckstone Av. EH10	41	L11
Buckstone Bk. EH10	41	L12
Buckstone Circle EH10	41	M11
Buckstone Clo. EH10	41	M11
Buckstone Ct. EH10	41	L11
Buckstone Cres. EH10	41	L12
Buckstone Crook EH10	41	M11
Buckstone Dell EH10	41	L12
Buckstone Dr. EH10	41	L12
Buckstone Gdns. EH10	41	L11
Buckstone Gate EH10	41	M11
Buckstone Grn. EH10	41	L11
Buckstone Gro. EH10	41	L12
Buckstone Hill EH10	41	L12
Buckstone Howe EH10	41	M11
Buckstone Lea EH10	41	M11
Buckstone Ln. EH10	41	L11
Buckstone Ln. E. EH10	41	M11
Buckstone Neuk EH10	41	M11
Buckstone Pl. EH10	41	L11
Buckstone Ri. EH10	41	M11
Buckstone Rd. EH10	41	L11
Buckstone Row EH10	41	M12
Buckstone Shaw EH10	41	M11
Buckstone Ter. EH10	41	L11
Buckstone Vw. EH10	41	L12
Buckstone Way EH10	41	L12
Buckstone Wd. EH10	41	L11
Buckstone Wynd EH10	41	M11
Buckstoneside EH10	41	M11
Buckstone Circle		
Bughtlin Dr. EH12	16	E17
Bughtlin Gdns. EH12	16	E16
Bughtlin Grn. EH12	16	E17
Bughtlin Ln. EH12	16	E16
Bughtlin Mkt. EH12	16	E17
Bughtlin Pk. EH12	16	E16
Bughtlin Pl. EH12	16	E17
Bull's Clo. EH8	7	N16
Burdiehouse Av. EH17	42	O10
Burdiehouse Cres. EH17	43	O10
Burdiehouse Crossway EH17	42	O10
Burdiehouse Dr. EH17	42	O10
Burdiehouse Ln. EH17	42	O10
Burdiehouse Medway EH17	42	O10
Burdiehouse Pl. EH17	42	O10
Burdiehouse Rd. EH17	42	O10
Burdiehouse Sq. EH17	42	O10
Burdiehouse St. EH17	42	O10
Burdiehouse Ter. EH17	42	O10
Burgess St. EH6	12	O19
Burgess Ter. EH9	33	O14
Burghlee Cres., Loanh. EH20	47	O8
Burghlee Ter., Loanh. EH20	47	P8
Burghtoft EH17	43	Q11
Burlington St. EH6	12	N19
Burnbank, Loanh. EH20	47	O8
Burnbank Cres., Loanh. EH20	47	O9
Burnbank Gro., Loanh. EH20	47	O9
Burnbrae EH12	16	E16
Burndene Dr. (Strait.), Loanh. EH20	47	N9
Burnhead Cres. EH16	42	O12
Burnhead Gro. EH16	42	O11
Burnhead Ln. EH16	42	O11
Burnhead Path E. EH16	42	O11
Burnhead Path W. EH16	42	O11
Burns St. EH6	12	O18
Burnside EH12	16	E16
Burnside Pk., Bal. EH14	44	B9
Bush St., Muss. EH21	24	U16
Bush Ter., Muss. EH21	24	U15
Cables Wynd EH6	12	N19
Caddell's Row EH4	8	E19
Cadiz St. EH6	12	O19
Cadogan Rd. EH16	42	O12
Cadzow Pl. EH7	21	O17
Caerketton Cotts. EH13	40	K12
Caerketton Ct. EH13	40	K12
Caerlaverock Ct. EH12	16	E16
Craigievar Wynd		
Cairds Row, Muss. EH21	24	U16
Cairnmuir Rd. EH12	17	G16
Cairns Dr., Bal. EH14	44	B8
Cairns Gdns., Bal. EH14	44	B8
Cairntows Clo. EH16	33	P14
Caithness Pl. EH5	11	L19
Caiy Stane EH10	41	L11
Caiyside EH10	41	L10
Caiystane Av. EH10	41	L11
Caiystane Cres. EH10	41	L11
Caiystane Dr. EH10	41	K11
Caiystane Gdns. EH10	41	K11
Caiystane Hill EH10	41	L11
Caiystane Ter. EH10	41	K11
Caiystane Vw. EH10	41	L11
Calder Ct. EH11	28	F13
Calder Cres. EH11	28	E13
Calder Dr. EH11	28	F13
Calder Gdns. EH11	28	E13
Calder Gro. EH11	28	F13
Calder Pk. EH11	28	F13
Calder Pl. EH11	28	F13
Calder Rd. EH11	29	G13
Calder Rd. Gdns. EH11	29	H14
Calder Vw. EH11	28	E13
Caledonian Cres. EH11	19	K15
Caledonian Pl. EH11	19	K15
Caledonian Rd. EH11	19	L15
Calton Hill EH1	7	N17
Calton Hill EH7	7	N17
Calton Rd. EH8	7	M16
Cambridge Av. EH6	12	N18
Cambridge Gdns. EH6	12	N18
Cambridge St. EH1	6	L16
Cambridge St. La. EH1	6	L16
Cambusnethan St. EH7	21	O17
Cameron Cres. EH16	33	O14
Cameron Ho. Av. EH16	33	O14
Cameron March EH16	33	O14
Cameron Pk. EH16	33	O14
Cameron Smail Rd. (Ricc.), Currie EH14	37	D12
Cameron Ter. EH16	33	O14
Cameron Toll EH16	33	O14
Cameron Toll Gdns. EH16	33	O14
Cammo Bk. EH4	16	E17
Cammo Brae EH4	16	E17
Cammo Cres. EH4	16	E17
Cammo Gdns. EH4	16	E17
Cammo Gro. EH4	15	D17
Cammo Hill EH4	15	D17
Cammo Parkway EH4	16	E17
Cammo Pl. EH4	16	E17
Cammo Rd. EH4	15	D17
Cammo Rd. EH12	15	C17
Cammo Wk. EH4	15	D17
Campbell Av. EH12	18	J16
Campbell Pk. Cres. EH13	39	G11
Campbell Pk. Dr. EH13	39	G11
Campbell Rd. EH12	18	J16
Campbell's Clo. EH8	7	N16
Calton Rd.		
Campie Ct., Muss. EH21	24	U15
Campie Gdns.		
Campie Gdns., Muss. EH21	24	U15
Campie La., Muss. EH21	24	U15
Campie Rd., Muss. EH21	24	U15
Campview (Dand.), Dalk. EH22	51	R12
Campview Av. (Dand.), Dalk. EH22	51	R12
Campview Cres. (Dand), Dalk. EH22	51	R12
Campview Gdns. (Dand.), Dalk. EH22	51	R12
Campview Gro. (Dand.), Dalk. EH22	51	S12
Campview Ter. (Dand.), Dalk. EH22	51	R12
Camus Av. EH10	41	L11
Camus Pk. EH10	41	L11
Camus Pl. E. EH10	41	L11
Camus Rd. E. EH10	41	L11
Camus Rd. W. EH10	41	L11
Canaan La. EH10	31	L14
Candlemaker Row EH1	7	M16
Candlemaker's Cres. EH17	43	Q11
Candlemaker's Pk. EH17	43	Q11
Canning St. EH3	6	L16
Canning St. La. EH3	6	L16
Cannon Wynd EH6	12	N19
Canon La. EH3	20	M17
Canon St. EH3	20	M17
Canongate EH8	7	N16
Canonmills EH3	11	M18
Capelaw Ct. EH13	40	K12
Capelaw Rd. EH13	39	H11
Captain's Dr. EH16	42	O11
Captain's Ln. EH16	42	O11
Captain's Rd. EH17	42	O11
Captain's Row EH16	42	O11
Carberry Pl. EH12	18	K16
Carberry Rd. (Inver.), Muss. EH21	25	V14
Carfrae Gdns. EH4	17	H17
Carfrae Gro. EH4	17	H17
Carfrae Pk. EH4	17	H17
Carfrae Rd. EH4	17	H17
Cargil Ct. EH5	11	L19
Cargil Ter. EH5	11	L19
Carlton St. EH4	6	L17
Carlton Ter. EH7	7	N17
Carlton Ter. Brae EH7	7	N17
Carlton Ter. La. EH7	7	N17
Carlton Ter. Ms. EH7	7	N17
Carlyle Pl. EH7	21	O17
Carlyle Pl., Muss. EH21	24	V15
Carnbee Av. EH16	43	P11
Carnbee Cres. EH16	43	P11
Carnbee Dell EH16	43	P11
Carnbee End EH16	43	P11
Carnbee Pk. EH16	43	P11
Carnegie Ct. EH8	7	N16
Carnegie St. EH8	7	N16
Carnethy Av. EH13	39	H11
Caroline Gdns. EH12	17	G16
Caroline Pk. EH5	10	J20
Caroline Pk. Av. EH5	10	J20
Caroline Pk. Gro. EH5	10	J19
Caroline Pl. EH12	17	G16
Caroline Ter. EH12	16	F16
Carpet La. EH6	12	O19
Bernard St.		
Carrick Cres. (Easth.), Dalk. EH22	50	V8
Carrick Knowe Av. EH12	29	G15
Carrick Knowe Dr. EH12	29	G15
Carrick Knowe Gdns. EH12	29	G15
Carrick Knowe Gro. EH12	29	G15
Carrick Knowe Hill EH12	29	G15
Carrick Knowe Ln. EH12	29	G15
Carrick Knowe Parkway EH12	29	G15
Carrick Knowe Pl. EH12	29	G15
Carrick Knowe Rd. EH12	29	G14
Carrick Knowe Ter. EH12	29	G15
Carrington Cres. EH4	10	K18
Crewe Rd. S.		
Carrington Rd. EH4	19	K17
Carron Pl. EH6	13	O19
Carrubber's Clo. EH1	7	M16
High St.		
Casselbank St. EH6	12	N18
Cassel's La. EH6	12	N18
Castle Av. EH12	29	F15
Castle Esp. EH1	6	M16
Castle St. EH2	6	L16
Castle Ter. EH1	6	L16
Castle Tor. EH3	6	L16
Castle Wynd N. EH1	20	M16
Castle Wynd S. EH1	20	M16
Johnston Ter.		
Castlehill FH1	6	M16
Castlelaw Rd. EH13	39	H11
Castleview Ho. EH17	33	P13
Cathcart Pl. EH11	19	K15
Cathedral La. EH1	7	M17
Catherine Pl. EH3	11	M18
Cattle Rd. EH14	30	H14
Causeway, The EH15	21	P15
Causewayside EH9	32	N15
Cavalry Pk. Dr. EH15	22	P15
Cedars, The EH13	40	H12
Cemetery Rd., Dalk. EH22	50	T10
Chalmers Bldgs. EH3	6	L15
Fountainbridge		
Chalmers Clo. EH1	7	M16
High St.		
Chalmers Cres. EH9	32	M15
Chalmers St. EH3	6	M15
Chamberlain Rd. EH10	31	L14
Chambers St. EH1	7	M16
Champigny Ct., Muss. EH21	25	W15
Chancelot Cres. EH6	11	M19
Chancelot Gro. EH5	11	M19
Chancelot Ter. EH6	11	M19
Chapel Ct. EH16	34	Q14
Chapel La. EH6	12	O19
Maritime St.		
Chapel St. EH8	7	N15

Name	Pg	Grid
Chapel Wynd EH1	6	M16
West Port		
Charles St. EH8	7	M16
Charles St. La. EH8	7	M16
Charlesfield EH8	7	M16
Bristo Sq.		
Charlotte La. EH2	6	L16
Charlotte Sq. EH2	6	L16
Charterhall Gro. EH9	32	M14
Charterhall Rd. EH9	32	M13
Chatterrig EH13	40	K12
Cherry Tree Av., Bal. EH14	45	D10
Cherry Tree Cres., Bal. EH14	45	C10
Cherry Tree Cres., Currie EH14	45	C10
Cherry Tree Gdns., Bal. EH14	45	C10
Cherry Tree Gro., Bal. EH14	45	C10
Cherry Tree Ln., Bal. EH14	45	D10
Cherry Tree Pk., Bal. EH14	45	C10
Cherry Tree Pl., Currie EH14	45	C10
Cherry Tree Vw., Bal. EH14	45	D10
Chessels Ct. EH8	7	N16
Chesser Av. EH14	30	H14
Chesser Cotts. EH11	30	H14
Gorgie Rd.		
Chesser Cres. EH14	30	J14
Chesser Gdns. EH14	30	H14
Chesser Gro. EH14	30	H14
Chesser Ln. EH14	30	H14
Chester St. EH3	19	L16
Chestnut St. EH5	10	K20
Cheyne St. EH4	19	L17
Christian Cres. EH15	23	R16
Christian Gro. EH15	23	R16
Christian Path EH15	22	R16
Christiemiller Av. EH7	22	Q17
Christiemiller Gro. EH7	22	Q17
Christiemiller Pl. EH7	22	Q17
Chuckie Pend EH3	6	L16
Church Hill EH10	31	L14
Church Hill Dr. EH10	31	L14
Church Hill Pl. EH10	31	L14
Church La., Muss. EH21	25	V15
Church Rd., Lass. EH18	48	Q9
Church St., Loanh. EH20	48	P8
Circle, The (Dand.), Dalk. EH22	51	R12
Circus Gdns. EH3	6	L17
Circus La. EH3	6	L17
Citadel Ct. EH6	12	N19
Citadel Pl. EH6	12	N19
Commercial St.		
Citadel St. EH6	12	N19
City of Edinburgh Bypass, The EH10	40	J11
City of Edinburgh Bypass, The EH12	27	D15
City of Edinburgh Bypass, The EH13	40	J11
City of Edinburgh Bypass, The EH14	38	F12
City of Edinburgh Bypass, The EH17	46	N10
City of Edinburgh Bypass, The, Lass. EH18	48	Q10
Clackmae Gro. EH16	42	N12
Clackmae Rd. EH16	42	N12
Clapper La. EH16	33	O13
Clapperton Pl. EH7	21	O17
Lower London St.		
Clarebank Cres. EH6	13	O18
Claremont Bk. EH7	20	M17
Claremont Ct. EH7	12	M18
Claremont Cres. EH7	12	M18
Claremont Gdns. EH6	13	O18
Claremont Gro. EH7	12	M18
Claremont Pk. EH6	13	O18
Claremont Rd. EH6	13	O18
Clarence St. EH3	19	L17
Clarendon Cres. EH4	6	L17
Clarinda Gdns., Dalk. EH22	50	V9
Clarinda Ter. EH16	33	O13
Clark Av. EH5	11	M19
Clark Pl. EH5	11	L19
Clark Rd. EH5	11	L19
Claverhouse Dr. EH16	42	O12
Clayhills Gro., Bal. EH14	44	B9
Clayhills Pk., Bal. EH14	44	B9
Clayknowes Av., Muss. EH21	24	U15
Clayknowes Ct., Muss. EH21	24	U14
Clayknowes Dr., Muss. EH21	24	T15
Clayknowes Pl., Muss. EH21	24	T15
Clayknowes Rd., Muss. EH21	24	U15
Clayknowes Way, Muss. EH21	24	U15
Clearburn Cres. EH16	33	O14
Clearburn Gdns. EH16	33	O14
Clearburn Rd. EH16	33	O14
Cleekim Dr. EH15	34	R14
Cleekim Rd. EH15	34	R14
Cleikiminfield EH15	35	R14
Cleikiminrig EH15	35	R14
Clerk St. EH8	20	N15
Clerk St., Loanh. EH20	47	P8
Clermiston Av. EH4	16	F17
Clermiston Cres. EH4	17	F17
Clermiston Dr. EH4	16	F17
Clermiston Gdns. EH4	17	F17
Clermiston Grn. EH4	16	F17
Clermiston Gro. EH4	17	F17
Clermiston Hill EH4	17	F17
Clermiston Ln. EH4	16	F17
Clermiston Medway EH4	17	F17
Clermiston Pk. EH4	17	F17
Clermiston Pl. EH4	17	F17
Clermiston Rd. EH12	17	G16
Clermiston Rd. N. EH4	17	G17
Clermiston Ter. EH12	17	G16
Clermiston Vw. EH4	17	G17
Clerwood Bk. EH12	16	F16
Clerwood Gdns. EH12	16	F16
Clerwood Gro. EH12	17	G16
Clerwood Ln. EH12	16	F16
Clerwood Pk. EH12	16	F16
Clerwood Pl. EH4	17	G16
Clerwood Row EH12	16	F16
Clerwood Ter. EH12	17	G16
Clerwood Vw. EH12	17	G16
Clerwood Way EH12	16	F16
Clifton Sq. EH15	22	R16
Baileyfield Rd.		
Clifton Ter. EH12	19	L16
Clinton Rd. EH9	31	L14
Clockmill La. EH8	21	O17
Clovenstone Dr. EH14	39	G12
Clovenstone Gdns. EH14	39	G12
Clovenstone Pk. EH14	39	G12
Clovenstone Rd. EH14	39	G12
Cluny Av. EH10	31	L13
Cluny Dr. EH10	31	L13
Cluny Gdns. EH10	31	L13
Cluny Pl. EH10	32	M13
Cluny Ter. EH10	31	L13
Clyde St. EH1	20	M17
Coalhill EH6	12	N19
Coates Cres. EH3	6	L16
Coates Gdns. EH12	19	K16
Coates Pl. EH3	19	L16
Coatfield La. EH6	12	O19
Cobbinshaw Ho. EH11	28	F13
Cobden Cres. EH9	32	N14
Cobden Rd. EH9	32	N14
Cobden Ter. EH11	19	L16
Coburg St. EH6	12	N19
Cochran Pl. EH7	20	M17
East London St.		
Cochran Ter. EH7	20	M17
Cochrane Pl. EH6	12	O18
Cockburn Cres., Bal. EH14	44	B8
Cockburn St. EH1	7	M16
Cockburnhill Rd., Bal. EH14	44	B8
Cockmylane EH10	41	K11
Coffin La. EH11	19	K15
Coillesdene Av. EH15	23	S16
Coillesdene Cres. EH15	23	S16
Coillesdene Dr. EH15	23	S16
Coillesdene Gdns. EH15	23	S16
Coillesdene Gro. EH15	23	S16
Coillesdene Ln. EH15	24	T16
Coillesdene Ter. EH15	23	S16
Coinyie Ho. Clo. EH1	7	N16
Blackfriars St.		
Colinton Gro. EH14	30	J13
Colinton Gro. W. EH14	30	J13
Colinton Mains Cres. EH13	40	J11
Colinton Mains Dr. EH13	40	J12
Colinton Mains Gdns. EH13	40	J12
Colinton Mains Grn. EH13	40	J12
Colinton Mains Gro. EH13	40	K12
Colinton Mains Ln. EH13	40	J12
Colinton Mains Pl. EH13	40	K12
Colinton Mains Rd. EH13	40	J12
Colinton Mains Ter. EH13	40	K12
Colinton Rd. EH10	31	K14
Colinton Rd. EH13	40	H12
Colinton Rd. EH14	30	J13
College Wynd EH1	7	M16
Cowgate		
Collins Pl. EH3	19	L17
Colmestone Gate EH10	41	L11
Coltbridge Av. EH12	18	J16
Coltbridge Gdns. EH12	18	K16
Coltbridge Millside EH12	18	J16
Coltbridge Av.		
Coltbridge Ter. EH12	18	J16
Coltbridge Vale EH12	18	K16
Columba Av. EH4	18	H17
Columba Rd. EH4	18	H17
Colville Pl. EH3	19	L17
Comely Bk. EH4	19	K17
Comely Bk. Av. EH4	19	L17
Comely Bk. Gro. EH4	19	K17
Comely Bk. Pl. EH4	19	L17
Comely Bk. Pl. Ms. EH4	19	L17
Comely Bk. Rd. EH4	19	K17
Comely Bk. Row EH4	19	L17
Comely Bk. St. EH4	19	K17
Comely Bk. Ter. EH4	19	L17
Comely Grn. Cres. EH7	21	O17
Comely Grn. Pl. EH7	21	O17
Comiston Dr. EH10	31	K13
Comiston Gdns. EH10	31	L13
Comiston Gro. EH10	41	L12
Comiston Pl. EH10	31	L13
Comiston Ri. EH10	41	L12
Comiston Rd. EH10	41	L12
Comiston Springs Av. EH10	41	L12
Comiston Ter. EH10	31	L13
Comiston Vw. EH10	41	L12
Commercial St. EH6	12	N19
Commercial Wf. EH6	12	O19
Connaught Pl. EH6	12	M19
Considine Gdns. EH8	21	P17
Considine Ter. EH8	21	P17
Constitution Pl. EH6	12	O19
Constitution St. EH6	12	O18
Convening Ct. EH4	19	K17
Dean Path		
Corbiehill Av. EH4	9	H18
Corbiehill Cres. EH4	9	G18
Corbiehill Gdns. EH4	9	H18
Corbiehill Gro. EH4	9	H18
Corbiehill Pk. EH4	9	G18
Corbiehill Pl. EH4	9	G18
Corbiehill Rd. EH4	9	G18
Corbiehill Ter. EH4	9	G18
Corbieshot EH15	35	R15
Cornhill Ter. EH6	13	O18
Cornwall St. EH1	6	L16
Cornwallis Pl. EH3	20	M17
Coronation Wk. EH3	20	M15
Corporation Bldgs. EH6	12	N19
Sheriff Brae		
Corrennie Dr. EH10	31	L13
Corrennie Gdns. EH10	31	L13
Corslet Cres., Currie EH14	38	E11
Corslet Pl., Currie EH14	38	E11
Corslet Rd., Currie EH14	38	E11
Corstorphine Bk. Av. EH12	16	F16
Corstorphine Bk. Dr. EH12	16	F16
Corstorphine Bk. Ter. EH12	16	F16
Corstorphine High St. EH12	16	F15
Corstorphine Hill Av. EH12	17	G16
Corstorphine Hill Cres. EH12	17	G16
Corstorphine Hill Gdns. EH12	17	G16
Corstorphine Hill Rd. EH12	17	G16
Corstorphine Ho. Av. EH12	17	G15
Corstorphine Ho. Ter. EH12	17	G15
Corstorphine Pk. Gdns. EH12	17	G15
Corstorphine Rd. EH12	17	H15
Cortleferry Dr., Dalk. EH22	49	T9
Cortleferry Gro., Dalk. EH22	49	T9
Cortleferry Pk., Dalk. EH22	49	T9
Cortleferry Ter., Dalk. EH22	49	T9
Corunna Pl. EH6	12	N19
Cottage Grn. EH4	8	E18
Cottage Homes EH13	40	H11
Cottage La., Muss. EH21	25	W15
Cottage Pk. EH4	17	H17
Couper St. EH6	12	N19
Cowan Rd. EH11	30	K14
Cowan's Clo. EH8	7	N15
Cowden Cres., Dalk. EH22	50	V10
Cowden Gro., Dalk. EH22	50	V10

Name	Page	Ref
Cowden La., Dalk. EH22	50	V10
Cowden Pk., Dalk. EH22	50	V10
Cowden Ter., Dalk. EH22	50	V10
Cowden Vw., Dalk. EH22	50	V10
Cowgate EH1	7	M16
Cowgatehead EH1	20	M16
Cowpits (White.), Muss. EH21	25	V13
Cowpits Rd.	25	V13
(White.), Muss. EH21		
Coxfield EH11	30	J14
Craigcrook Av. EH4	17	H17
Craigcrook Gdns. EH4	18	H17
Craigcrook Gro. EH4	17	H17
Craigcrook Pk. EH4	17	H17
Craigcrook Pl. EH4	18	H17
Craigcrook Rd. EH4	17	G17
Craigcrook Sq. EH4	17	H17
Craigcrook Ter. EH4	18	H17
Craigend Pk. EH16	33	P13
Craigentinny Av. EH7	22	Q17
Craigentinny Av. N. EH6	13	P18
Craigentinny Cres. EH7	22	Q17
Craigentinny Gro. EH7	22	Q17
Craigentinny Pl. EH7	22	Q17
Craigentinny Rd. EH7	22	P17
Craighall Av. EH6	11	M19
Craighall Bk. EH6	11	M19
Craighall Cres. EH6	11	M19
Craighall Gdns. EH6	11	M19
Craighall Rd. EH6	11	M19
Craighall Ter. EH6	11	M19
Craighall Ter., Muss. EH21	25	W15
Craighill Gdns. EH10	31	K13
Craighouse Av. EH10	31	K13
Craighouse Gdns. EH10	31	K13
Craighouse Pk. EH10	31	K13
Craighouse Rd. EH10	31	K13
Craighouse Ter. EH10	31	K13
Craigievar Ct. EH12	16	E16
Craigievar Wynd		
Craigievar Sq. EH12	16	E16
Craigievar Wynd EH12	16	E16
Craiglea Dr. EH10	31	K13
Craiglea Pl. EH10	31	K13
Craigleith Av. N. EH4	18	J16
Craigleith Av. S. EH4	18	J16
Craigleith Bk. EH4	18	J17
Craigleith Cres. EH4	18	J17
Craigleith Dr. EH4	18	J17
Craigleith Gdns. EH4	18	J17
Craigleith Gro. EH4	18	J17
Craigleith Hill EH4	18	J17
Craigleith Hill Av. EH4	18	J17
Craigleith Hill Cres. EH4	18	J17
Craigleith Hill Gdns. EH4	18	J17
Craigleith Hill Grn. EH4	18	J17
Craigleith Hill Gro. EH4	18	J17
Craigleith Hill Ln. EH4	18	J17
Craigleith Hill Pk. EH4	18	J17
Craigleith Hill Row EH4	18	J17
Craigleith Ri. EH4	18	J16
Craigleith Rd. EH4	18	J17
Craigleith Vw. EH4	18	J16
Craiglockhart Av. EH14	30	J13
Craiglockhart Bk. EH14	30	J13
Craiglockhart Cres. EH14	30	J13
Craiglockhart Dell Rd. EH14	30	J13
Craiglockhart Dr. N. EH14	30	J13
Craiglockhart Dr. S. EH14	30	J13
Craiglockhart Gdns. EH14	30	J13
Craiglockhart Gro. EH14	40	J12
Craiglockhart Ln. EH14	30	J13
Craiglockhart Pk. EH14	30	J13
Craiglockhart Pl. EH14	30	J13
Craiglockhart Quad. EH14	30	J13
Craiglockhart Rd. EH14	30	J13
Craiglockhart Rd. N. EH14	30	J13
Craiglockhart Ter. EH14	30	K14
Craiglockhart Vw. EH14	30	J13
Craigmillar Castle Av. EH16	34	P14
Craigmillar Castle Gdns. EH16	33	P14
Craigmillar Castle Gro. EH16	34	P14
Craigmillar Castle Ln. EH16	34	Q14
Craigmillar Castle Rd. EH16	34	P14
Craigmillar Castle Ter. EH16	34	P14
Craigmillar Pk. EH16	33	P14
Craigmount Pk. EH16	33	N14
Craigmount App. EH12	16	F16
Craigmount Av. EH12	16	F16
Craigmount Av. N. EH4	16	E17
Craigmount Av. N. EH12	16	E17
Craigmount Bk. EH4	16	E17
Craigmount Bk. W. EH4	16	E17
Craigmount Brae EH12	16	E17
Craigmount Ct. EH4	16	E17
Craigmount Cres. EH12	16	E16
Craigmount Dr. EH12	16	E16
Craigmount Gdns. EH12	16	E16
Craigmount Gro. EH12	16	E16
Craigmount Gro. N. EH12	16	E16
Craigmount Hill EH4	16	E17
Craigmount Ln. EH12	16	E16
Craigmount Pk. EH12	16	E16
Craigmount Pl. EH12	16	E16
Craigmount Ter. EH12	16	E16
Craigmount Vw. EH12	16	E16
Craigmount Way EH12	16	F17
Craigour Av. EH17	43	Q12
Craigour Cres. EH17	43	Q12
Craigour Dr. EH17	43	Q12
Craigour Gdns. EH17	43	Q12
Craigour Grn. EH17	43	P12
Craigour Gro. EH17	43	Q12
Craigour Ln. EH17	43	Q12
Craigour Pl. EH17	43	P12
Craigour Ter. EH17	43	Q12
Craigs Av. EH12	16	E15
Craigs Bk. EH12	16	E16
Craigs Cres. EH12	16	E16
Craigs Dr. EH12	16	E16
Craigs Gdns. EH12	16	E16
Craigs Gro. EH12	16	F16
Craigs Ln. EH12	16	F16
Craigs Pk. EH12	16	E16
Craigs Rd. EH12	16	E16
Crame Ter., Dalk. EH22	49	T9
Cramond Av. EH4	8	E19
Cramond Bk. EH4	8	E19
Cramond Bri. EH4	8	D18
Cramond Bri. Cotts. EH4	8	D18
Queensferry Rd.		
Cramond Brig Toll EH4	8	D18
Cramond Cres. EH4	8	E19
Cramond Gdns. EH4	8	E19
Cramond Glebe Gdns. EH4	8	F19
Cramond Glebe Rd. EH4	8	E20
Cramond Glebe Ter. EH4	8	E20
Cramond Grn. EH4	8	E19
Cramond Gro. EH4	8	E19
Cramond Pk. EH4	8	E19
Cramond Pl. EH4	8	F19
Cramond Regis EH4	8	E18
Cramond Rd. N. EH4	8	F19
Cramond Rd. S. EH4	9	F19
Cramond Ter. EH4	8	E19
Cramond Vale EH4	8	E19
Cramond Village EH4	8	E20
Cranston St. EH8	7	N16
Crarae Av. EH4	18	J16
Craufurdland EH4	8	E18
Crawford Bri. EH7	21	O17
Bothwell St.		
Crawfurd Rd. EH16	33	N14
Crescent, The EH10	31	L13
Crescent, The EH11	30	H14
Gorgie Rd.		
Crewe Bk. EH5	10	K19
Crewe Cres. EH5	10	J19
Crewe Gro. EH5	10	K19
Crewe Ln. EH5	10	J19
Crewe Path EH5	10	J19
Crewe Pl. EH5	10	J19
Crewe Rd. Gdns. EH5	10	J19
Crewe Rd. N. EH5	10	J19
Crewe Rd. S. EH4	10	K18
Crewe Rd. W. EH5	10	J19
Crewe Ter. EH5	10	J19
Crewe Toll EH4	10	J18
Crichton St. EH8	7	M16
Crighton Pl. EH7	12	N18
Croall Pl. EH7	20	N17
Croft St., Dalk. EH22	50	U10
Croft-an-righ EH8	21	N17
Cromwell Pl. EH6	12	N19
Crookston Rd.	25	W14
(Inver.), Muss. EH21		
Cross Rd., Loanh. EH20	47	N8
Crosswood Av., Bal. EH14	44	B8
Crosswood Cres., Bal. EH14	44	B8
Crown Pl. EH6	12	N18
Crown St. EH6	12	N18
Cuddy La. EH10	31	L14
Cuguen Pl., Lass. EH18	49	R9
Cultins Rd. EH11	28	E14
Cumberland St. EH3	6	M17
Cumberland St. N. E. La. EH3	20	M17
Cumberland St. N. W. La. EH3	20	M17
Cumberland St. S. E. La. EH3	20	M17
Cumberland St. S. W. La. EH3	6	M17
Cumin Pl. EH9	32	N15
Cumlodden Av. EH12	18	J16
Cumnor Cres. EH16	33	O13
Cunningham Pl. EH6	12	N18
Curriehill Castle Dr., Bal. EH14	45	C10
Curriehill Rd., Currie EH14	37	C12
Currievale Dr., Currie EH14	37	D10
Currievale Pk., Currie EH14	37	D10
Currievale Pk. Gro., Currie EH14	37	D10
Daiches Braes EH15	23	S15
Dairsie Pl. EH7	21	O17
Stanley Pl.		
Daisy Ter. EH11	30	K15
Merchiston Gro.		
Dalgety Av. EH7	21	O17
Dalgety Rd. EH7	21	O17
Dalgety St. EH7	21	O17
Dalhousie Rd., Dalk. EH22	50	T9
Dalhousie Ter. EH10	31	L13
Dalkeith Rd. EH16	32	N15
Dalkeith St. EH15	23	S16
Dalkeith Western Bypass, Dalk. EH22	49	S10
Dalkeith Western Bypass, Lass. EH18	49	S10
Dalmahoy Cres., Bal. EH14	44	B10
Dalmahoy Rd. (Ratho), Newbr. EH28	26	A13
Dalmeny Rd. EH6	12	M19
Dalmeny St. EH6	12	N18
Dalry Pl. EH11	19	L16
Dalry Rd. EH11	19	K15
Dalry Rd. La. EH11	19	K15
Dalry Rd.		
Dalrymple Cres. EH9	32	N14
Dalrymple Cres., Muss. EH21	24	U15
Dalrymple Ln., Muss. EH21	25	V15
Dalum Ct., Loanh. EH20	47	O8
Dalum Dr., Loanh. EH20	47	O8
Dalum Gro., Loanh. EH20	47	O8
Dalum Ln., Loanh. EH20	47	O8
Dalziel Pl. EH7	21	O17
London Rd.		
Damhead EH10	46	M8
Damside EH4	19	K16
Danderhall Cres.	51	R12
(Dand.), Dalk. EH22		
Danube St. EH4	6	L17
Darling's Bldgs. EH3	19	L17
Saunders St.		
Darnaway St. EH3	6	L17
Darnell Hd. EH5	11	L19
Davidson Gdns. EH4	9	H18
Davidson Pk. EH4	10	J18
Davidson Rd. EH4	10	J18
Davie St. EH8	7	N16
Dean Bk. La. EH3	19	L17
Dean Bri. EH3	6	L17
Dean Bri. EH4	6	L17
Dean Pk. Cres. EH4	19	L17
Dean Pk. Ms. EH4	6	L17
Dean Pk. St. EH4	6	L17
Dean Path EH4	19	K17
Dean Path Bldgs. EH4	19	K17
Dean Path		
Dean St. EH4	6	L17
Dean Ter. EH4	6	L17
Deanery Clo. EH7	21	P17
Deanhaugh St. EH4	6	L17
Deanpark Av., Bal. EH14	44	C9
Deanpark Bk., Bal. EH14	45	C9
Deanpark Brae, Bal. EH14	45	C9
Deanpark Ct., Bal. EH14	44	B9
Deanpark Cres., Bal. EH14	45	C9
Deanpark Gdns., Bal. EH14	45	C9
Deanpark Gro., Bal. EH14	45	C9
Deanpark Pl., Bal. EH14	44	C9
Deanpark Sq., Bal. EH14	44	C9
Dechmont Rd. EH12	16	E16
Delhaig EH11	30	J14
Dell Rd. EH13	39	H12
Delta Pl. (Inver.), Muss. EH21	25	V14

Name	Page	Grid
Denham Grn. Av. EH5	11	L19
Denham Grn. Pl. EH5	11	L19
Denham Grn. Ter. EH5	11	L19
Denholm Rd., Muss. EH21	24	T15
Denholm Way, Muss. EH21	24	T14
Derby St. EH6	11	M19
Devon Pl. EH12	19	K16
Dewar Pl. EH3	6	L16
Dewar Pl. La. EH3	6	L16
Dick Pl. EH9	32	M14
Dickson St. EH6	12	N18
Dickson's Clo. EH1	7	M16
High St.		
Dickson's Ct. EH8	7	M16
Bristo Sq.		
Dinmont Dr. EH16	33	O13
Distillery La. EH11	19	L16
Dalry Rd.		
Dobbie's Av., Bonny. EH19	49	R8
Dobbie's Rd., Lass. EH18	49	R8
Dochart Dr. EH4	16	F17
Dock Pl. EH6	12	N19
Dock St. EH6	12	N19
Dolphin Av., Currie EH14	37	D10
Dolphin Gdns. E., Currie EH14	37	D10
Dolphin Gdns. W., Currie EH14	37	D10
Dolphin Rd., Currie EH14	37	D10
Dorset Pl. EH11	19	L15
Double Dykes	25	V14
(Inver.), Muss. EH21		
Double Hedges Pk. EH16	33	O13
Double Hedges Rd. EH16	33	O13
Douglas Cres. EH12	19	K16
Douglas Cres., Bonny. EH19	49	R8
Douglas Gdns. EH4	19	K16
Douglas Gdns. Ms. EH4	19	K16
Douglas Ter. EH11	19	L16
Doune Ter. EH3	6	L17
Dovecot Gro. EH14	29	H13
Dovecot Ln. EH14	29	H13
Dovecot Pk. EH14	39	H12
Dovecot Rd. EH12	29	F15
Dowie's Mill La. EH4	8	D18
Downfield Pl. EH11	19	K15
Downie Gro. EH12	17	G15
Downie Pl., Muss. EH21	25	V15
Downie Ter. EH12	17	G15
Dreghorn Av. EH13	40	K11
Dreghorn Dr. EH13	40	K11
Dreghorn Gdns. EH13	40	K11
Dreghorn Gro. EH13	40	K11
Dreghorn Link EH13	40	K11
Dreghorn Ln. EH13	39	H11
Dreghorn Pk. EH13	40	J11
Dreghorn Pl. EH13	40	K11
Drum Av. EH17	43	Q11
Drum Brae Av. EH12	16	F16
Drum Brae Cres. EH4	16	F17
Drum Brae Dr. EH4	16	F17
Drum Brae Gdns. EH12	16	F16
Drum Brae Gro. EH4	16	F17
Drum Brae Neuk EH12	16	F16
Drum Brae N. EH4	16	E17
Drum Brae Pk. EH12	16	F16
Drum Brae Pk. App. EH12	16	F16
Drum Brae Pl. EH12	16	F16
Drum Brae S. EH12	16	F16
Drum Brae Ter. EH4	16	F17
Drum Brae Wk. EH4	16	E17
Drum Cotts. EH17	43	Q11
Drum Cres. EH17	43	Q11
Drum Pk. Yd. EH7	21	O17
Drum Vw. Av.	51	R12
(Dand.), Dalk. EH22		
Drumdryan St. EH3	6	L15
Drummond Pl. EH3	6	M17
Drummond St. EH8	7	N16
Drumsheugh Gdns. EH3	6	L16
Drumsheugh Pl. EH3	6	L16
Queensferry St.		
Dryden Av., Loanh. EH20	47	O8
Dryden Cres., Loanh. EH20	47	O8
Dryden Gdns. EH7	12	N18
Dryden Glen, Loanh. EH20	47	N8
Dryden Pl. EH9	32	N15
Dryden Rd., Loanh. EH20	47	N8
Dryden St. EH7	12	N18
Dryden Ter. EH7	12	N18
Dryden Ter., Loanh. EH20	47	O8
Dryden Vw., Loanh. EH20	47	O8
Drylaw Av. EH4	18	J17
Drylaw Cres. EH4	18	H17
Drylaw Gdns. EH4	10	H18
Drylaw Grn. EH4	18	H17
Drylaw Gro. EH4	18	H17
Drylaw Ho. Gdns. EH4	10	H18
Drylaw Ho. Paddock EH4	10	H18
Duart Cres. EH4	16	F17
Dublin Meuse EH3	6	M17
Dublin St. EH1	7	M17
Dublin St. EH3	7	M17
Dublin St. La. EH3	7	M17
Dublin St. La. S. EH1	7	M17
Duddingston Av. EH15	22	Q15
Duddingston Cres. EH15	22	R15
Duddingston Gdns. N. EH15	22	Q16
Duddingston Gdns. S. EH15	22	Q15
Duddingston Gro. E. EH15	22	Q16
Duddingston Gro. W. EH15	22	Q15
Duddingston Ln. EH15	22	Q15
Duddingston Mains Cotts. EH15	22	R15
Milton Rd.		
Duddingston Mills EH8	22	Q16
Duddingston Pk. EH15	22	R16
Duddingston Pk. S. EH15	34	R15
Duddingston Ri. EH15	22	Q15
Duddingston Rd. EH15	22	Q16
Duddingston Rd. W. EH15	22	P15
Duddingston Rd. W. EH16	33	P15
Duddingston Row EH15	22	Q15
Duddingston Sq. E. EH15	22	Q15
Duddingston Sq. W. EH15	22	Q16
Duddingston Vw. EH15	22	Q15
Duddingston Yards EH15	34	R15
Duddingston Pk. S.		
Dudley Av. EH6	12	M19
Dudley Av. S. EH6	12	N19
Dudley Bk. EH6	12	M19
Dudley Cres. EH6	12	M19
Dudley Gdns. EH6	12	M19
Dudley Gro. EH6	12	M19
Dudley Ter. EH6	12	M19
Duff St. EH11	19	K15
Duff St. La. EH11	19	K15
Duke Pl. EH6	12	O18
Duke St. EH6	12	O18
Duke St., Dalk. EH22	50	U10
Duke's Wk. EH8	21	O17
Dumbiedykes Rd. EH8	7	N16
Dumbryden Dr. EH14	29	G13
Dumbryden Gdns. EH14	29	G13
Dumbryden Gro. EH14	29	G13
Dumbryden Rd. EH14	29	G13
Dun-ard Gdn. EH9	32	M14
Dunbar St. EH3	6	L16
Duncan Pl. EH6	12	O18
Duncan St. EH9	32	N14
Duncans Gait EH14	29	G13
Dundas Cres., Dalk. EH22	50	T9
Dundas Gro., Dalk. EH22	50	T9
Dundas Pk., Bonny. EH19	49	S8
Dundas Rd., Dalk. EH22	50	T9
Dundas St. EH3	6	M17
Dundas St., Bonny. EH19	49	R8
Dundee St. EH11	19	K15
Dundee Ter. EH11	19	K15
Dundonald St. EH3	20	M17
Dundrennan Cotts. EH16	33	P13
Dunedin St. EH7	12	M18
Dunlop's Ct. EH1	6	M16
Grassmarket		
Dunollie Ct. EH12	16	E16
Craigievar Wynd		
Dunrobin Pl. EH3	19	L17
Dunsmuir Ct. EH12	16	F15
Dunsyre Ho. EH11	28	F13
Dunvegan Ct. EH4	8	E18
Durar Dr. EH4	16	F17
Durham Av. EH15	22	Q16
Durham Dr. EH15	22	R15
Durham Gdns. N. EH15	22	R16
Durham Gdns. S. EH15	22	R15
Durham Gro. EH15	22	R16
Durham Pl. EH3	20	M17
Dundas St.		
Durham Pl. E. EH15	22	R16
Durham Pl. La. EH15	22	R16
Durham Pl. W. EH15	22	Q15
Durham Rd. EH15	22	R16
Durham Rd. S. EH15	22	R15
Durham Sq. EH15	22	Q16
Durham Ter. EH15	22	Q16
Durward Gro. EH16	33	O13
Earl Grey St. EH3	6	L16
Earl Haig Gdns. EH5	11	L19
Earl Haig Homes EH11	29	H14
Earlston Pl. EH7	21	O17
East Adam St. EH8	7	N16
East Barnton Av. EH4	9	G18
East Barnton Gdns. EH4	9	G18
East Brighton Cres. EH15	22	R16
East Broughton Pl. EH1	20	M17
Broughton Pl.		
East Caiystane Pl. EH10	41	L11
East Caiystane Rd. EH10	41	L11
East Castle Rd. EH10	31	L15
East Champanyie EH9	32	N14
East Clapperfield EH16	33	O13
East Claremont St. EH7	20	M17
East Comiston EH10	41	L11
East Ct. EH4	18	J17
East Ct. EH16	34	Q14
East Cft.	26	A13
(Ratho), Newbr. EH28		
East Cromwell St. EH6	12	N19
East Crosscauseway EH8	7	N15
East Fm. of Gilmerton EH17	43	Q11
East Fettes Av. EH4	11	K18
East Fountainbridge EH3	6	L16
East Hannahfield, Bal. EH14	44	B9
East Hermitage Pl. EH6	12	O18
East Lillypot EH5	11	L19
East London St. EH7	20	M17
East Mkt. St. EH8	7	N16
East Mayfield EH9	32	N14
East Montgomery Pl. EH7	20	N17
East Newington Pl. EH9	32	N15
East Norton Pl. EH7	21	N17
East Parkside EH16	20	N15
East Preston St. EH8	20	N15
East Preston St. La. EH8	20	N15
East Preston St.		
East Restalrig Ter. EH6	12	O18
East Savile Rd. EH16	32	N14
East Sciennes St. EH9	20	N15
East Scotland St. La. EH3	20	M17
East Silvermills La. EH3	19	L17
East Suffolk Rd. EH16	33	O14
East Telferton EH7	22	Q17
East Trinity Rd. EH5	11	L19
East Way, The EH8	22	Q16
Easter Belmont Rd. EH12	18	H16
Easter Currie Ct., Currie EH14	38	E10
Easter Currie Cres., Currie EH14	38	E11
Easter Currie Pl., Currie EH14	38	E11
Easter Currie Ter., Currie EH14	38	E10
Easter Drylaw Av. EH4	10	J18
Easter Drylaw Bk. EH4	10	J18
Easter Drylaw Dr. EH4	10	J18
Easter Drylaw Gro. EH4	10	J18
Easter Drylaw Ln. EH4	10	J18
Easter Drylaw Pl. EH4	10	J18
Easter Drylaw Vw. EH4	10	J18
Easter Drylaw Way EH4	10	J18
Easter Haugh EH13	40	K12
Easter Hermitage EH6	13	O18
Easter Pk. Dr. EH4	9	G18
Easter Rd. EH6	12	O18
Easter Rd. EH7	21	N17
Easter Steil EH10	31	K13
Easter Warriston EH7	11	M18
Eastfield EH15	24	T16
Eastfield Gdns. EH15	24	T16
Eastfield Pl. EH15	24	T16
Eastfield Rd., Newbr. EH28	14	B15
Easthouses Ind. Est.	50	V8
Easthouses Ct., Dalk. EH22	50	V8
Easthouses Pl.	50	V8
(Easth.), Dalk. EH22		
Easthouses Rd.	50	V9
(Easth.), Dalk. EH22		

Street	Page	Grid
Easthouses Way	50	V9
(Easth.), Dalk. EH22		
Eden La. EH10	31	L14
Eden Ter. EH10	31	L14
Newbattle Ter.		
Edenhall Bk., Muss. EH21	25	W15
Edenhall Cres., Muss. EH21	25	W15
Edenhall Rd., Muss. EH21	25	W15
Edgefield Ind. Est., Loanh. EH20	47	P9
Edgefield Pl., Loanh. EH20	47	P8
Edgefield Rd., Loanh. EH20	47	P9
Edina Pl. EH7	21	O17
Edina St. EH7	20	N17
Edinburgh Airport EH12	14	A16
Edinburgh Pk. EH12	27	D15
Edinburgh Rd., Dalk. EH22	50	T10
Edinburgh Rd., Muss. EH21	24	T16
Edmonstone Av.	51	R12
(Dand.), Dalk. EH22		
Edmonstone Dr.	51	R12
(Dand.), Dalk. EH22		
Edmonstone Rd.	51	R12
(Dand.), Dalk. EH22		
Edmonstone Ter.	51	R12
(Dand.), Dalk. EH22		
Eglinton Cres. EH12	19	K16
Eglinton St. EH12	19	K16
Egypt Ms. EH10	32	M14
Eildon St. EH3	11	M18
Eildon Ter. EH3	11	L18
Elbe St. EH6	12	O19
Elcho Ter. EH15	23	S16
Elder St. EH1	7	M17
Elder St. E. EH1	7	M17
Eldindean Pl., Bonny. EH19	49	R8
Eldindean Rd., Bonny. EH19	49	R8
Eldindean Ter., Bonny. EH19	49	R8
Electra Pl. EH15	22	R17
Elgin Pl. EH12	19	K16
Elgin St. N. EH7	20	N17
Elgin St. S. EH7	20	N17
Elgin Ter. EH7	20	N17
Elizafield EH6	12	N18
Ellangowan Ter. EH16	33	O13
Ellen's Glen Rd. EH17	43	P11
Ellersly Rd. EH12	18	J16
Elliot Gdns. EH14	40	J12
Elliot Pk. EH14	40	J12
Elliot Pl. EH14	40	J12
Elliot Rd. EH14	40	J12
Elliot St. EH7	20	N17
Elm Pl. EH6	12	O18
Elm Row EH7	7	N17
Elm Row, Lass. EH18	49	R9
Elmfield Ct., Dalk. EH22	50	U10
Elmfield Pk., Dalk. EH22	50	U10
Elmfield Rd., Dalk. EH22	50	U10
Elmwood Ter. EH6	13	O18
Eltringham Gdns. EH14	30	J14
Eltringham Gro. EH14	30	J14
Eltringham Ter. EH14	30	J14
Engine Rds., Loanh. EH20	47	P8
Erskine Pl. EH2	6	L16
Shandwick Pl.		
Esdaile EH9	32	M14
Esk Glades, Dalk. EH22	50	U10
Esk Pl., Dalk. EH22	50	T10
Eskbank Ct., Dalk. EH22	50	T10
Eskbank Rd., Bonny. EH19	49	S8
Eskbank Rd., Dalk. EH22	50	T9
Eskbank Ter., Dalk. EH22	50	T9
Eskdaill Ct., Dalk. EH22	50	U10
South St.		
Eskdaill St., Dalk. EH22	50	U10
Eskdale Ct., Bonny. EH19	49	R8
Eskdale Dr., Bonny. EH19	48	R8
Eskdale Ms., Muss. EH21	25	V15
Eskdale Ter., Bonny. EH19	49	R8
Eskfield Gro., Dalk. EH22	49	S9
Eskmill Vills., Muss. EH21	24	U15
Eskside Ct., Dalk. EH22	50	T10
Ironmills Rd.		
Eskside E., Muss. EH21	25	V15
Eskside W., Muss. EH21	24	U15
Eskview Av., Muss. EH21	24	U15
Eskview Cres., Muss. EH21	24	U15
Eskview Gro., Dalk. EH22	50	T10
Eskview Gro., Muss. EH21	24	U15
Eskview Rd., Muss. EH21	24	U15
Eskview Ter., Muss. EH21	24	U15
Eskview Vills., Dalk. EH22	50	T9
Esplanade EH4	8	F20
Esplanade Ter. EH15	23	S16
Essendean Pl. EH4	16	F17
Essendean Ter. EH4	16	F17
Essex Brae EH4	8	E18
Essex Pk. EH4	8	E18
Essex Rd. EH4	8	E18
Esslemont Rd. EH16	32	N13
Ethel Ter. EH10	31	L13
Eton Ter. EH4	6	L17
Ettrick Gro. EH10	31	L15
Ettrick Rd. EH10	31	K14
Ettrickdale Pl. EH3	19	L17
Eva Pl. EH9	32	N13
Evans Gdns., Bonny. EH19	49	S8
Ewerland EH4	8	E18
Eyre Cres. EH3	20	M17
Eyre Pl. EH3	20	M17
Eyre Ter. EH3	20	M17
Fair-a-Far EH4	8	E19
Fair-a-Far Cotts. EH4	8	E19
Fair-a-Far Shot EH4	8	E19
Fairford Gdns. EH16	33	O13
Fairhaven Vills., Dalk. EH22	50	T9
Fairmile Av. EH10	41	L11
Fairview Rd., Newbr. EH28	14	A16
Fairways	24	U14
(Monk.), Muss. EH21		
Fala Ct. EH16	43	O11
Falcon Av. EH10	31	L14
Falcon Ct. EH10	31	L14
Falcon Gdns. EH10	31	L14
Falcon Rd. EH10	31	L14
Falcon Rd. W. EH10	31	L14
Falkland Gdns. EH12	17	G17
Farrer Gro. EH7	22	Q17
Farrer Ter. EH7	22	Q17
Fauldburn EH12	16	E17
Fauldburn Pk. EH12	16	E17
Featherhall Av. EH12	16	F15
Featherhall Cres. N. EH12	16	F15
Featherhall Cres. S. EH12	16	F15
Featherhall Gro. EH12	16	F15
Featherhall Pl. EH12	16	F15
Featherhall Rd. EH12	16	F15
Featherhall Ter. EH12	16	F15
Ferguson Ct., Muss. EH21	24	V14
Ferguson Dr., Muss. EH21	24	U14
Ferguson Gdns., Muss. EH21	24	U14
Ferguson Dr.		
Ferguson Grn., Muss. EH21	24	U14
Ferguson Vw., Muss. EH21	24	U14
Ferniehill Av. EH17	43	Q11
Ferniehill Dr. EH17	43	Q11
Ferniehill Gdns. EH17	43	Q12
Ferniehill Gro. EH17	43	Q12
Ferniehill Pl. EH17	43	Q11
Ferniehill Rd. EH17	43	Q11
Ferniehill Sq. EH17	43	Q11
Ferniehill St. EH17	43	Q12
Ferniehill Ter. EH17	43	Q11
Ferniehill Way EH17	43	Q12
Fernielaw Av. EH13	39	H11
Fernieside Av. EH17	43	Q12
Fernieside Cres. EH17	43	Q12
Fernieside Dr. EH17	43	Q12
Fernieside Gdns. EH17	43	Q12
Fernieside Gro. EH17	43	Q12
Ferry Rd. EH4	10	H18
Ferry Rd. EH5	10	K18
Ferry Rd. EH6	12	M19
Ferry Rd. Av. EH4	10	J18
Ferry Rd. Dr. EH4	10	J19
Ferry Rd. Gdns. EH4	10	J18
Ferry Rd. Gro. EH4	10	J18
Ferry Rd. Pl. EH4	10	J18
Ferryfield EH5	11	K19
Festival Sq. EH3	6	L16
Fettes Av. EH4	19	K17
Fettes Ri. EH4	11	K18
Fettes Row EH3	20	M17
Fidra Ct. EH4	9	H19
Figgate Bk. EH15	23	R17
Figgate La. EH15	22	R17
Figgate St. EH15	22	R17
Fillyside Av. EH7	22	Q17
Fillyside Rd. EH7	13	Q18
Fillyside Ter. EH7	13	Q18
Findhorn Pl. EH9	32	N14
Findlay Av. EH7	13	P18
Findlay Cotts. EH7	13	P18
Findlay Gdns. EH7	13	P18
Findlay Gro. EH7	13	P18
Findlay Medway EH7	13	P18
Fingal Pl. EH9	20	M15
Fingzies Pl. EH6	12	O18
Finlaggan Ct. EH12	16	E16
Craigievar Wynd		
Firrhill Cres. EH13	40	K12
Firrhill Dr. EH13	40	K12
Firrhill Ln. EH13	40	K12
First Gait	37	D12
(Ricc.), Currie EH14		
Fishers Wynd, Muss. EH21	24	U15
Fishmarket Sq. EH6	11	M20
Fishwives Causeway EH15	22	Q17
Fleshmarket Clo. EH1	7	M16
High St.		
Forbes Rd. EH10	31	L15
Forbes St. EH8	7	N15
Fords Rd. EH11	30	H14
Forres St. EH3	6	L17
Forrest Hill EH1	7	M16
Forrest Rd. EH1	7	M16
Forrester Pk. Av. EH12	28	F14
Forrester Pk. Dr. EH12	28	F14
Forrester Pk. Gdns. EH12	28	F14
Forrester Pk. Grn. EH12	29	G14
Forrester Pk. Gro. EH12	29	F14
Forrester Pk. Ln. EH12	29	F14
Forrester Rd. EH12	16	F16
Forteviot Ho. EH17	43	P12
Forth St. EH1	7	M17
Forth Vw. Av., Currie EH14	37	D10
Forth Vw. Cres.	51	R12
(Dand.), Dalk. EH22		
Forth Vw. Rd., Currie EH14	37	D10
Forthview Cres., Currie EH14	37	D10
Forthview Rd. EH4	18	J17
Forthview Ter. EH4	18	H17
Foulis Cres., Jun.Grn. EH14	39	F11
Foundry La., Loanh. EH20	48	P9
Fountain Pl., Loanh. EH20	47	P8
Fountainbridge EH3	6	L15
Fountainhall Rd. EH9	32	N14
Fourth Gait	37	D12
(Ricc.), Currie EH14		
Fowler Cres., Loanh. EH20	48	P8
Fowler Sq., Loanh. EH20	48	P8
Fowler Ter. EH11	31	K15
Fox Covert Av. EH12	17	G17
Fox Covert Gro. EH12	17	G17
Fox Spring Cres. EH10	40	K12
Fox Spring Ri. EH10	41	L12
Fraser Av. EH5	11	L19
Fraser Cres. EH5	11	L19
Fraser Gdns. EH5	11	L19
Fraser Gro. EH5	11	L19
Fraser Homes EH13	39	H12
Spylaw Dk. Ru.		
Frederick St. EH2	6	M17
Freelands Rd.	26	B14
(Ratho), Newbr. EH28		
Frogston Av. EH10	41	L11
Frogston Gdns. EH10	41	L11
Frogston Gro. EH10	41	M11
Frogston Rd. E. EH17	42	N10
Frogston Rd. W. EH10	41	L11
Frogston Ter. EH10	41	M11
Gabriel's Rd. EH2	7	M17
West Register St.		
Gabriel's Rd. EH3	19	L17
Galachlaw Shot EH10	41	M11
Galachlawside EH10	41	M11
Gallolee, The EH13	40	J11
Galt Av., Muss. EH21	25	X15
Galt Cres., Muss. EH21	25	X15
Gamekeeper's Ln. EH4	8	E19
Gamekeeper's Pk. EH4	8	E19
Gamekeeper's Rd. EH4	8	E19
Garden Ter. EH4	9	F18
Gardiner Gro. EH4	18	H17
Gardiner Rd. EH4	18	H17
Gardiner Ter. EH4	18	H17
Gardner St. EH7	21	O17
Lower London Rd.		
Gardner's Cres. EH3	6	L16
Garscube Ter. EH12	18	J16
Garvald Ct. EH16	42	O11

Name	Page	Grid
Gayfield Clo. EH1	20	N17
Gayfield Sq.		
Gayfield Pl. EH7	20	N17
Gayfield Pl. La. EH1	20	N17
Gayfield Sq. EH1	20	N17
Gayfield St. EH1	20	N17
Gaynor Av., Loanh. EH20	47	O8
General's Entry EH8	7	M16
Bristo Sq.		
George Av., Loanh. EH20	47	O8
George Cres., Loanh. EH20	47	P8
George Dr., Loanh. EH20	47	O8
George IV Bri. EH1	7	M16
George Sq. EH8	7	M15
George Sq. La. EH8	7	M15
George St. EH2	6	L16
George Ter., Loanh. EH20	47	O8
Gibb's Entry EH8	7	N16
Simon Sq.		
Gibraltar Ct., Dalk. EH22	50	U10
Gibraltar Gdns., Dalk. EH22	50	U10
Gibraltar Rd., Dalk. EH22	50	U10
Gibraltar Ter., Dalk. EH22	50	U10
Gibson Dr., Dalk. EH22	50	V10
Gibson St. EH7	12	N18
Gibson Ter. EH11	19	L15
Gifford Pk. EH8	7	N15
Gilberstoun EH15	23	S15
Gilberstoun Brig EH15	35	S15
Gilberstoun Ln. EH15	35	S15
Gilberstoun Pl. EH15	23	S15
Gilberstoun Wynd EH15	35	S15
Gilchrist's Entry EH1	20	M17
Leith St.		
Gilchrist's La. EH1	7	N17
Greenside Row		
Giles St. EH6	12	N19
Gillespie Cres. EH10	19	L15
Gillespie Pl. EH10	19	L15
Gillespie Rd. EH13	39	G11
Gillespie St. EH3	19	L15
Gillsland Pk. EH10	31	K14
Gillsland Rd. EH10	31	K14
Gilmerton Dykes Av. EH17	43	P11
Gilmerton Dykes Cres. EH17	43	P11
Gilmerton Dykes Dr. EH17	43	P11
Gilmerton Dykes Gdns. EH17	43	P11
Gilmerton Dykes Gro. EH17	43	P11
Gilmerton Dykes Ln. EH17	43	P11
Gilmerton Dykes Pl. EH17	43	P11
Gilmerton Dykes Rd. EH17	43	P10
Gilmerton Dykes St. EH17	43	P11
Gilmerton Dykes Ter. EH17	43	P11
Gilmerton Dykes Vw. EH17	43	P11
Gilmerton Pl. EH17	43	P11
Gilmerton Rd. EH16	33	O13
Gilmerton Rd. EH17	43	P12
Gilmerton Rd., Dalk. EH22	49	S10
Gilmerton Rd., Lass. EH18	51	Q11
Gilmerton Sta. Rd. EH17	43	Q10
Gilmore Pk. EH3	6	L15
Gilmore Pl. EH3	6	L15
Gilmore Pl. La. EH3	6	L15
Gilmour Rd. EH16	32	N14
Gilmour St. EH8	7	N16
Gilmour's Entry EH8	7	N16
Gilmour St.		
Gladstone Pl. EH6	13	O18
Gladstone Ter. EH9	20	N15
Glanville Pl. EH3	6	L17
Kerr St.		
Glasgow Rd. EH12	16	E15
Glasgow Rd., Newbr. EH28	14	A15
Glebe, The EH4	8	E19
Glebe Gdns. EH12	17	F15
Glebe Gro. EH12	17	F15
Glebe Pl. EH1	7	M16
High St.		
Glebe Pl., Lass. EH18	48	Q9
Glebe Rd. EH12	17	F15
Glebe St., Dalk. EH22	50	U10
Glebe Ter. EH12	17	F15
Glen St. EH3	6	M15
Glenallan Dr. EH16	33	O13
Glenallan Ln. EH16	33	O13
Glenalmond Ct. EH11	29	F13
Glenbrook, Bal. EH14	44	A8
Glenbrook Rd., Bal. EH14	44	A8
Glencairn Cres. EH12	19	K16
Glendevon Av. EH12	18	H15
Glendevon Gdns. EH12	18	H15
Glendevon Gro. EH12	18	H15
Glendevon Pk. EH12	18	H15
Glendevon Pl. EH12	18	H15
Glendevon Rd. EH12	18	H15
Glendevon Ter. EH12	18	H15
Glendinning Cres. EH16	42	O12
Glenesk Cres., Dalk. EH22	50	T9
Glenfinlas St. EH3	6	L16
Glengyle Ter. EH3	19	L15
Glenisla Gdns. EH9	32	M14
Glenisla Gdns. La. EH9	32	M14
Glenisla Gdns.		
Glenlea Cotts. EH11	30	J14
Glenlee Av. EH8	21	P16
Glenlee Gdns. EH8	21	P16
Glenlockhart Bk. EH14	30	J13
Glenlockhart Rd. EH10	30	J13
Glenlockhart Rd. EH14	30	J13
Glenlockhart Valley EH14	30	J13
Glenogle Pl. EH3	19	L17
Glenogle Rd. EH3	19	L17
Glenogle Ter. EH3	11	L18
Glenorchy Pl. EH1	7	N17
Greenside Row		
Glenorchy Ter. EH9	32	N14
Glenpark, Bal. EH14	44	A9
Glenure Ln. EH4	16	F17
Glenvarloch Cres. EH16	42	O12
Gloucester La. EH3	6	L17
Gloucester Pl. EH3	6	L17
Gloucester Sq. EH3	6	L17
Gloucester La.		
Gloucester St. EH3	6	L17
Goff Av. EH7	22	Q17
Gogar Mains Fm. Rd. EH12	15	C16
Gogar Sta. Rd. EH12	27	C15
Gogarbank EH12	27	D14
Gogarloch Haugh EH12	28	E15
Gogarloch Muir EH12	28	E15
Gogarloch Rd. EH12	28	E15
Gogarloch Syke EH12	28	E15
Gogarside Roundabout EH12	15	D15
Gogarstone Rd., Newbr. EH28	26	B15
Goldenacre Ter. EH3	11	L18
Goldie Ter., Loanh. EH20	47	O8
Golf Course Rd., Bonny. EH19	49	R8
Goose Grn. Av., Muss. EH21	25	V16
Goose Grn. Bri., Muss. EH21	25	V16
Goose Grn. Cres., Muss. EH21	25	V16
Goose Grn. Pl., Muss. EH21	25	V16
Goose Grn. Rd., Muss. EH21	25	V16
Gordon Ln. EH12	17	G16
Gordon Rd. EH12	17	G16
Gordon St. EH6	12	O18
Gordon Ter. EH16	33	O13
Gorgie Cotts. EH11	30	J14
Gorgie Pk. Clo. EH14	30	J14
Gorgie Pk. Rd. EH14	30	J14
Gorgie Rd. EH11	30	J15
Gosford Pl. EH6	12	M19
Gowanhill Rd., Currie EH14	36	B11
Gracefield Ct., Muss. EH21	24	U15
Fishers Wynd		
Gracemount Dr. EH16	42	O12
Gracemount Dr. EH16	42	O11
Gracemount Pl. EH16	42	O11
Gracemount Rd. EH16	42	O11
Gracemount Sq. EH16	42	O11
Graham St. EH6	12	N19
Granby Rd. EH16	32	N14
Grandfield EH6	11	M19
Grandville EH6	11	M19
Grange Ct. EH9	32	N15
Causewayside		
Grange Cres. EH9	32	M14
Grange Ln. EH9	32	M14
Grange Ln. Gdns. EH9	32	M14
Grange Rd. EH9	32	M15
Grange Ter. EH9	32	M14
Grant Av. EH13	39	H11
Granton Cres. EH5	10	K19
Granton Gdns. EH5	11	K19
Granton Gro. EH5	11	K19
Granton Mains Av. EH4	10	J19
Granton Mains Bk. EH4	10	J19
Granton Mains Brae EH4	10	J19
Granton Mains Ct. EH4	10	J19
Granton Mains E. EH4	10	J19
Granton Mains Gait EH4	10	J19
Granton Mains Vale EH4	10	J19
Granton Mains Wynd EH4	10	J19
Granton Medway EH5	10	K19
Granton Pk. Av. EH5	10	K20
Granton Pl. EH5	11	K19
Granton Rd. EH5	11	L19
Granton Sq. EH5	11	K20
Granton Ter. EH5	11	K19
Granton Vw. EH5	11	K19
Grantully Pl. EH9	32	N14
Granville Ter. EH10	31	L15
Grassmarket EH1	6	M16
Grays Ct. EH8	7	N16
Gray's Ln. EH10	31	K14
Great Cannon Bk. EH15	22	R17
Great Carleton Pl. EH16	34	R14
Great Carleton Sq. EH16	34	R14
Great Junct. St. EH6	12	N19
Great King St. EH3	6	M17
Great Michael Clo. EH6	12	M20
Newhaven Pl.		
Great Michael Ri. EH6	12	M19
Great Michael Sq. EH4	9	G18
Main St.		
Great Stuart St. EH3	6	L16
Green, The EH4	9	G18
Green, The, Bal. EH14	45	C8
Green St. EH7	20	M17
Green Way EH14	29	G13
Greenbank Av. EH10	31	L13
Greenbank Cres. EH10	41	L12
Greenbank Dr. EH10	31	K13
Greenbank Gdns. EH10	41	K12
Greenbank Gro. EH10	40	K12
Greenbank La. EH10	31	K13
Greenbank Ln. EH10	41	K12
Greenbank Pk. EH10	40	K12
Greenbank Pl. EH10	31	L13
Greenbank Ri. EH10	41	K12
Greenbank Rd. EH10	31	K13
Greenbank Row EH10	40	K12
Greenbank Ter. EH10	31	L13
Greendykes Av. EH16	34	Q14
Greendykes Dr. EH16	34	Q14
Greendykes Gdns. EH16	34	Q14
Greendykes Ho. EH16	34	Q14
Greendykes Ln. EH16	34	Q14
Greendykes Rd. EH16	34	Q14
Greendykes Ter. EH16	34	Q14
Greenend Dr. EH17	43	P12
Greenend Gdns. EH17	43	P12
Greenend Gro. EH17	43	P12
Greenfield Cres., Bal. EH14	45	C8
Greenfield Pk.		
(Monk.), Muss. EH21		
Greenfield Rd., Bal. EH14	45	C8
Greenhill Ct. EH10	31	L15
Greenhill Gdns. EH10	31	L15
Greenhill Pk. EH10	31	L14
Greenhill Pl. EH10	31	L14
Greenhill Ter. EH10	31	L15
Greenlaw Hedge EH13	40	K12
Greenlaw Rig EH13	40	K12
Greenmantle Ln. EH16	33	O13
Greenside Ct. EH1	7	N17
Greenside Row		
Greenside La. EH1	7	N17
Greenside Pl. EH1	7	N17
Greenside Row EH1	7	N17
Greyfriars Pl. EH1	7	M16
Candlemaker Row		
Grierson Av. EH5	11	L19
Grierson Cres. EH5	11	L19
Grierson Gdns. EH5	11	L19
Grierson Rd. EH5	11	K19
Grierson Sq. EH5	11	L19
Grierson Vills. EH5	11	L19
Grigor Av. EH4	10	J18
Grigor Dr. EH4	10	J18
Grigor Gdns. EH4	10	J18
Grigor Ter. EH4	10	J18
Grindlay St. EH3	6	L16
Grindlay St. Ct. EH3	6	L16
Groathill Av. EH4	18	J17
Groathill Gdns. E. EH4	18	J17
Groathill Gdns. W. EH4	18	J17
Groathill Rd. N. EH4	10	J18
Groathill Rd. S. EH4	18	J17
Grosvenor Cres. EH12	19	K16
Grosvenor Gdns. EH12	19	K16
Grosvenor St. EH12	19	L16

Name	Page	Grid
Latch Pk. EH13	40	J12
Lauder Ln. EH9	32	M14
Lauder Rd. EH9	32	M15
Lauder Rd., Dalk. EH22	50	U9
Lauderdale St. EH9	32	M15
Laurel Bk., Dalk. EH22	50	V9
Laurel Ter. EH11	31	K15
Laurie St. EH6	12	O18
Lauriston Fm. Rd. EH4	9	G18
Lauriston Gdns. EH3	6	M16
Lauriston Pk. EH3	6	M15
Lauriston Pl. EH3	6	M16
Lauriston St. EH3	6	M16
Lauriston Ter. EH3	6	M16
Laverockbank Av. EH5	11	M19
Laverockbank Cres. EH5	11	M19
Laverockbank Gdns. EH5	11	M19
Laverockbank Gro. EH5	11	M19
Laverockbank Rd. EH5	11	M19
Laverockbank Ter. EH5	11	M19
Laverockdale Cres. EH13	39	H11
Laverockdale Ln. EH13	39	H11
Laverockdale Pk. EH13	39	H11
Law Pl. EH15	22	R17
Pipe St.		
Lawnmarket EH1	7	M16
Lawrie Ter., Loanh. EH20	47	O8
Leadervale Rd. EH16	42	N12
Leadervale Ter. EH16	42	N12
Leamington Pl. EH10	31	L15
Leamington Ter.		
Leamington Rd. EH10	19	L15
Leamington Ter. EH10	19	L15
Learmonth Av. EH4	19	K17
Learmonth Ct. EH4	19	K17
Learmonth Cres. EH4	19	K17
Learmonth Gdns. EH4	19	K17
Learmonth Gdns. La. EH4	19	K17
Learmonth Gdns. Ms. EH4	19	L17
Learmonth Gro. EH4	19	K17
Learmonth Pk. EH4	19	K17
Learmonth Pl. EH4	19	K17
Learmonth Ter. EH4	19	K17
Learmonth Ter. La. EH4	19	K17
Learmonth Vw. EH4	19	K17
Learmonth Ter.		
Lee Cres. EH15	22	R16
Leith Docks EH6	12	N20
Leith Links EH6	12	O18
Leith St. EH1	7	M17
Leith St. Ter. EH1	7	M17
Leith St.		
Leith Wk. EH6	12	N18
Leith Wk. EH7	7	N17
Lennel Av. EH12	18	J16
Lennox Row EH5	11	L19
Lennox St. EH4	6	L17
Lennox St. La. EH4	6	L17
Lennymuir EH12	14	B17
Leopold Pl. EH7	7	N17
Leslie Pl. EH4	6	L17
Leven Clo. EH3	19	L15
Leven St.		
Leven Ter. EH3	6	M15
Lewis Ter. EH11	19	L16
Lewisvale Av., Muss. EH21	25	W15
Lewisvale Ct., Muss. EH21	25	W15
Leyden Pk., Bonny. EH19	49	R8
Leyden Pl., Bonny. EH19	49	R8
Liberton Brae EH16	33	O12
Liberton Dr. EH16	42	N12
Liberton Gdns. EH16	42	O11
Liberton Pl. EH16	42	O12
Liberton Rd. EH16	33	O13
Liddesdale Pl. EH3	19	L17
Lily Ter. EH11	30	K14
Shandon Pl.		
Lilyhill Ter. EH8	21	P17
Limefield EH17	43	Q11
Limes, The EH17	31	L14
Lindean Pl. EH6	13	O18
Linden Pl., Loanh. EH20	48	P8
Lindsay Pl. EH1	7	M16
Chambers St.		
Lindsay Pl. EH6	12	N19
Lindsay Rd. EH6	12	N19
Lindsay St. EH6	12	N19
Linkfield Ct., Muss. EH21	25	W15
Linkfield Rd., Muss. EH21	25	V15
Links Av., Muss. EH21	24	U16
Links Gdns. EH6	13	O19
Links Gdns. La. EH6	13	O19
Links La. EH6	12	O19
Links Pl. EH6	12	O19
Links St., Muss. EH21	25	V15
Links Vw., Muss. EH21	24	U16
Lismore Av. EH8	21	P17
Lismore Cres. EH8	21	P17
Little Acre, Dalk. EH22	50	V8
Little France Ho. EH17	43	P12
Little France Mills EH16	34	P13
Little King St. EH1	7	M17
Little Rd. EH16	42	O12
Livingstone Pl. EH9	20	M15
Lixmount Av. EH5	11	M19
Lixmount Gdns. EH5	11	M19
Loan, The, Loanh. EH20	47	O8
Loanhead Rd.	47	O9
(Strait.), Loanh. EH20		
Loaning Cres. EH7	21	P17
Loaning Rd. EH7	21	P17
Loch Rd. EH4	17	H17
Lochend Av. EH7	13	O18
Lochend Castle Barns EH7	21	O17
Lochend Clo. EH8	7	N16
Canongate		
Lochend Cres. EH7	21	P17
Lochend Dr. EH7	21	O17
Lochend Gdns. EH7	21	O17
Lochend Gro. EH7	21	P17
Lochend Pk. EH7	21	O17
Lochend Quad. EH7	21	P17
Lochend Rd. EH6	12	O18
Lochend Rd. EH7	12	O18
Lochend Rd. N.,	24	U15
Muss. EH21		
Lochend Rd. S. EH7	21	O17
Lochend Rd. S., Muss. EH21	24	U15
Lochend Sq. EH7	21	O17
Lochrin Bldgs. EH3	19	L15
Lochrin Pl. EH3	6	L15
Lochrin Ter. EH3	6	L15
Thornybauk		
Lochside Av. EH12	27	D15
Lochside Cres. EH12	27	D15
Lochview Ct. EH8	7	N16
Lockerby Cotts. EH16	43	P11
Lockerby Cres. EH16	43	P11
Lockerby Gro. EH16	43	P11
Lockharton Av. EH14	30	J13
Lockharton Cres. EH14	30	K13
Lockharton Gdns. EH14	30	K14
Logan St. EH3	20	M17
Loganlea Av. EH7	21	P17
Loganlea Dr. EH7	21	P17
Loganlea Gdns. EH7	21	P17
Loganlea Ln. EH7	21	P17
Loganlea Pl. EH7	21	P17
Loganlea Rd. EH7	21	P17
Loganlea Ter. EH7	21	P17
Logie Grn. Gdns. EH7	11	M18
Logie Grn. Ln. EH7	11	M18
Logie Grn. Rd. EH7	11	M18
Logie Mill EH7	11	M18
Lomond Rd. EH5	11	L19
Lomond Wk., Loanh. EH20	47	O9
London Rd. EH7	7	N17
London Rd. EH8	21	O17
London Rd., Dalk. EH22	50	U10
London St. EH3	20	M17
Long Craig Rigg EH5	10	J20
Long Craig Rd. EH5	10	J20
Long Dalmahoy Rd., Bal. EH14	37	C11
Longformacus Rd. EH16	42	O12
Longstone Av. EH14	29	H13
Longstone Cotts. EH14	29	H13
Longstone Rd.		
Longstone Cres. EH14	29	H14
Longstone Gdns. EH14	29	G14
Longstone Gro. EH14	29	H13
Longstone Pk. EH14	29	H13
Longstone Rd. EH14	29	G13
Longstone St. EH14	29	H13
Longstone Ter. EH14	29	G14
Longstone Vw. EH14	29	G14
Lonsdale Ter. EH3	6	M15
Lord Russell Pl. EH9	32	N15
Causewayside		
Loretto Ct., Muss. EH21	24	U14
Lorne Gro.	47	O9
(Strait.), Loanh. EH20		
Lorne Pl. EH6	12	N18
Lorne Sq. EH6	12	N18
Lorne St. EH6	12	N18
Lothian Bk., Dalk. EH22	50	T9
Lothian Dr.	50	V8
(Easth.), Dalk. EH22		
Lothian Rd. EH1	6	L16
Lothian Rd. EH3	6	L16
Lothian Rd., Dalk. EH22	50	U10
Lothian St. EH1	7	M16
Lothian St., Bonny. EH19	49	S8
Lothian St., Dalk. EH22	50	U10
Lothianburn EH10	46	M10
Lovedale Av., Bal. EH14	44	B9
Lovedale Cres., Bal. EH14	44	B9
Lovedale Gdns., Bal. EH14	44	B9
Lovedale Gro., Bal. EH14	44	B9
Lovedale Rd., Bal. EH14	44	C9
Lovers' Ln. EH9	32	M15
Lower Broomieknowe,	49	R8
Lass. EH18		
Lower Gilmore Pl. EH3	6	L15
Lower Granton Rd. EH5	11	K20
Lower Joppa EH15	23	S16
Lower London Rd. EH7	21	O17
Lufra Bk. EH5	11	L19
Lugton Brae, Dalk. EH22	50	T10
Lussielaw Rd. EH9	32	N13
Lutton Pl. EH8	20	N15
Lygon Rd. EH16	32	N13
Lyne St. EH7	21	O17
Lynedoch Pl. EH3	6	L16
Lynedoch Pl. La. EH3	6	L16
Macbeth Moir Rd., Muss.	25	X15
EH21		
MacDowall Rd. EH9	32	N14
Mackenzie Pl. EH3	6	L17
Madeira Pl. EH6	12	N19
Madeira St. EH6	12	N19
Magdala Cres. EH12	19	K16
Magdala Ms. EH12	19	K16
Magdalene Av. EH15	23	R15
Magdalene Ct. EH15	22	R15
Magdalene Dr. EH15	23	R15
Magdalene Gdns. EH15	23	R15
Magdalene Ln. EH15	23	R15
Magdalene Medway EH15	23	R15
Magdalene Pl. EH15	23	R15
Maidencraig Ct. EH4	18	J17
Maidencraig Cres. EH4	18	J17
Maidencraig Gro. EH4	18	J17
Main Point EH3	20	M16
Main St. (David.) EH4	9	G18
Main St., Bal. EH14	45	C9
Mains of Craigmillar EH16	34	P13
Maitland Av., Muss. EH21	24	U15
Maitland Pk. Rd., Muss. EH21	24	U15
Maitland St., Muss. EH21	24	U15
Mall Av., Muss. EH21	25	V15
Malleny Av., Bal. EH14	45	C9
Malleny Millgate, Bal. EH14	45	C8
Malta Grn. EH4	19	L17
St. Bernard's Row		
Malta Ter. EH4	19	L17
Manderston St. EH6	12	N18
Mannering Pl. EH16	42	O12
Manor Pl. EH3	19	L16
Manse Rd. EH12	17	F15
Manse St. EH12	16	F15
Mansfield Av., Muss. EH21	25	V15
Mansfield Ct., Muss. EH21	25	V15
Mansfield Pl. EH3	20	M17
Mansfield Pl., Muss. EH21	25	V15
Mansfield Rd., Bal. EH14	45	C9
Mansfield Rd., Muss. EH21	25	V15
Mansionhouse Rd. EH9	32	M15
March Gro. EH4	17	H17
March Pines EH4	17	G17
March Rd. EH4	17	G17
Marchbank Dr., Bal. EH14	45	C8
Marchbank Gdns., Bal. EH14	45	C8
Marchbank Gro., Bal. EH14	45	C8
Marchbank Pl., Bal. EH14	45	C8
Marchbank Way, Bal. EH14	45	C9
Marchfield Gdns. EH4	9	G18
Hillhouse Rd.		
Marchfield Gro. EH4	9	H18
Marchfield Pk. EH4	9	G18
Marchfield Pk. La. EH4	9	G18
Marchfield Ter. EH4	17	H17

Mountcastle Cres. EH8	22	Q16
Mountcastle Dr. N. EH8	22	Q16
Mountcastle Dr. N. EH15	22	Q16
Mountcastle Dr. S. EH15	22	Q16
Mountcastle Gdns. EH8	22	Q16
Mountcastle Grn. EH8	22	Q16
Mountcastle Gro. EH8	22	Q16
Mountcastle Ln. EH8	22	Q16
Mountcastle Pk. EH8	22	Q16
Mountcastle Cres.		
Mountcastle Pl. EH8	22	Q17
Mountcastle Ter. EH8	22	Q16
Mounthooly Ln. EH10	41	M11
Mountjoy Ter., Muss. EH21	25	V16
Mucklets Av., Muss. EH21	24	U14
Mucklets Ct., Muss. EH21	24	U14
Mucklets Cres., Muss. EH21	24	U14
Mucklets Dr., Muss. EH21	24	U14
Mucklets Pl., Muss. EH21	24	U14
Muir Wd. Cres., Currie EH14	38	E11
Muir Wd. Dr., Currie EH14	38	E11
Muir Wd. Gro., Currie EH14	38	E11
Muir Wd. Pl., Currie EH14	38	E11
Muir Wd. Rd., Currie EH14	38	E11
Muirdale Ter. EH4	18	H17
Muirend Av., Jun.Grn. EH14	39	G12
Muirfield Gdns., Loanh. EH20	47	P8
Muirhouse Av. EH4	10	H18
Muirhouse Bk. EH4	9	H18
Muirhouse Cres. EH4	10	H19
Muirhouse Dr. EH4	9	H19
Muirhouse Gdns. EH4	9	H19
Muirhouse Grn. EH4	9	H18
Muirhouse Gro. EH4	9	H19
Muirhouse Ln. EH4	9	H19
Muirhouse Medway EH4	9	H18
Muirhouse Pk. EH4	9	H18
Muirhouse Parkway EH4	9	H19
Muirhouse Pl. E. EH4	10	H18
Muirhouse Pl. W. EH4	10	H18
Muirhouse Ter. EH4	9	H18
Muirhouse Vw. EH4	9	H19
Muirhouse Way EH4	10	H18
Muirpark, Dalk. EH22	50	T9
Muirside EH13	40	K11
Mulberry Pl. EH6	12	M19
Newhaven Rd.		
Munro Dr. EH13	39	H11
Munro Pl. EH3	11	M18
Canonmills		
Murano Pl. EH7	20	N17
Murdoch Ter. EH11	19	L15
Murieston Cres. EH11	19	K15
Murieston Cres. La. EH11	19	K15
Murieston La. EH11	19	K15
Murieston Pl. EH11	19	K15
Murieston Rd. EH11	19	K15
Murieston Ter. EH11	19	K15
Murray Cotts. EH12	16	F15
Murrayburn App. EH14	28	F13
Murrayburn Dr. EH14	28	F13
Murrayburn Gdns. EH14	29	G13
Murrayburn Gate EH14	28	F13
Murrayburn Grn. EH14	29	G13
Murrayburn Gro. EH14	29	G13
Murrayburn Pk. EH14	29	F13
Murrayburn Pl. EH14	29	F13
Murrayburn Rd. EH14	29	F13
Murrayfield Av. EH12	18	J16
Murrayfield Dr. EH12	18	J16
Murrayfield Gdns. EH12	18	J16
Murrayfield Pl. EH12	18	J16
Murrayfield Rd. EH12	18	J16
Murrays, The EH17	43	P10
Murrays Brae, The EH17	43	P10
Musselburgh Rd. EH15	23	S16
Musselburgh Rd., Dalk. EH22	50	U10
Myreside Ct. EH10	31	K13
Myreside Rd. EH10	31	K14
Myrtle Ter. EH11	30	K15
Nantwich Dr. EH7	13	Q18
Napier Rd. EH10	31	K14
Neidpath Ct. EH12	16	E16
Craigievar Wynd		
Nellfield EH16	43	O12
Nelson Pl. EH3	6	M17
Dublin Meuse		
Nelson St. EH3	6	M17
Nether Craigour EH17	34	P13
Nether Craigwell EH8	7	N16
Nether Currie Cres., Currie EH14	38	E11
Nether Currie Pl., Currie EH14	38	E11
Nether Currie Rd., Currie EH14	38	E11
Nether Lennie EH12	15	C18
Netherbank EH16	42	N11
Netherbank Vw. EH16	42	N11
Netherby Rd. EH5	11	L19
New Arthur Pl. EH8	7	N16
New Belfield EH8	22	Q16
New Bells Ct. EH6	12	O19
New Broompark EH5	10	K20
New Broughton EH3	7	M17
New John's Pl. EH8	7	N15
New Lairdship Pl. EH11	29	F14
New Lairdship Yards EH11	29	F14
New La. EH6	12	M19
New Mart Rd. EH14	30	H14
New Meadowspott, Dalk. EH22	50	T9
Waverley Rd.		
New Morrison St. EH3	6	L16
New Orchardfield EH6	12	N18
New Skinners Clo. EH1	7	N16
Blackfriars St.		
New St. EH8	7	N16
New St. EH17	43	P11
New St., Muss. EH21	24	U15
New Swanston EH10	40	K11
New Twr. Pl. EH15	22	R17
Figgate La.		
Newbattle Abbey Cres., Dalk. EH22	50	T8
Newbattle Rd., Dalk. EH22	50	T9
Newbattle Ter. EH10	31	L14
Newbigging, Muss. EH21	25	V15
Newcraighall Dr. (Newcr.), Muss. EH21	35	S14
Newcraighall Rd. EH15	35	R14
Newcraighall Rd., Muss. EH21	35	S14
Newhailes Av., Muss. EH21	24	U15
Newhailes Cres., Muss. EH21	24	T15
Newhailes Rd., Muss. EH21	24	T15
Newhaven Main St. EH6	11	M20
Newhaven Pl. EH6	12	M20
Newhaven Rd. EH6	12	M19
Newington Rd. EH9	32	N15
Newkirkgate EH6	12	N19
Newlands Pk. EH9	32	N14
Mayfield Gdns.		
Newmarket Rd. EH14	30	J14
Newmills Av., Bal. EH14	45	C10
Newmills Cres., Bal. EH14	45	C10
Newmills Gro., Bal. EH14	45	C10
Newmills Rd., Bal. EH14	45	C10
Newmills Rd., Dalk. EH22	50	U10
Newmills Ter., Dalk. EH22	50	U10
James Lean Av.		
Newtoft St. EH17	43	Q11
Newton Ch. Rd. (Dand.), Dalk. EH22	51	R12
Newton St. EH11	30	K15
Newton St. (Easth.), Dalk. EH22	50	V0
Newton Village, Dalk. EH22	51	S12
Nicolson Sq. EH8	7	N16
Nicolson St. EH8	7	N16
Niddrie Cotts. EH15	35	S14
Niddrie Fm. Gro. EH16	34	Q14
Niddrie Ho. Av. EH16	34	Q14
Niddrie Ho. Dr. EH16	34	R14
Niddrie Ho. Gdns. EH16	34	R14
Niddrie Ho. Gro. EH16	34	R14
Niddrie Ho. Pk. EH16	34	Q14
Niddrie Ho. Sq. EH16	34	R14
Niddrie Ho. Pk.		
Niddrie Mains Ct. EH16	34	R14
Niddrie Mains Dr. EH16	34	Q14
Niddrie Mains Rd. EH15	34	Q14
Niddrie Mains Rd. EH16	34	P14
Niddrie Mains Ter. EH16	34	Q14
Niddrie Marischal Cres. EH16	34	Q14
Niddrie Marischal Dr. EH16	34	Q14
Niddrie Marischal Gdns. EH16	34	Q14
Niddrie Marischal Grn. EH16	34	Q14
Niddrie Marischal Gro. EH16	34	R14
Niddrie Marischal Ln. EH16	34	R14
Niddrie Marischal Pl. EH16	34	Q14
Niddrie Marischal Rd. EH16	34	R14
Niddrie Marischal St. EH16	34	Q14
Niddrie Mill Av. EH15	34	R14
Niddrie Mill Cres. EH15	34	R15
Niddrie Mill Dr. EH15	34	R14
Niddrie Mill Gro. EH15	34	R14
Niddrie Mill Pl. EH15	34	R14
Niddrie Mill Ter. EH15	34	R14
Niddry St. EH1	7	M16
Niddry St. S. EH1	7	M16
Cowgate		
Nigel Ln. EH16	42	O12
Nile Gro. EH10	31	L14
Nisbet Ct. EH7	13	O18
Niven's Knowe Rd., Loanh. EH20	47	N8
Nivensknowe Caravan Pk., Loanh. EH20	47	N8
Noble Pl. EH6	13	O18
North Bk. St. EH1	20	M16
North Bri. EH1	7	M16
North Bri. Arc. EH1	7	M16
North Bri.		
North Bughtlin Bk. EH12	16	E17
North Bughtlin Brae EH12	16	E17
North Bughtlin Gate EH12	16	E17
North Bughtlin Neuk EH12	16	E17
North Bughtlin Pl. EH12	16	E17
North Bughtlin Rd. EH12	16	E17
North Bughtlinfield EH12	16	E17
North Bughtlinrig EH12	16	E17
North Bughtlinside EH12	16	E17
North Cairntow EH16	33	P15
North Castle St. EH2	6	L17
North Charlotte St. EH2	6	L16
North E. Circ. Pl. EH3	6	L17
North Fort St. EH6	12	N19
North Grns. EH15	34	R15
North Gyle Av. EH12	16	E15
North Gyle Dr. EH12	16	E16
North Gyle Fm. Ct. EH12	16	E15
North Gyle Fm. La. EH12	16	E15
North Gyle Gro. EH12	16	E15
North Gyle Ln. EH12	16	E16
North Gyle Pk. EH12	16	E16
North Gyle Rd. EH12	16	E16
North Gyle Ter. EH12	16	E15
North High St., Muss. EH21	24	U15
North Hillhousefield EH6	12	N19
North Junct. St. EH6	12	N19
North Leith Mill EH6	12	N19
North Leith Sands EH6	12	N19
North Meadow Wk. EH3	6	M15
North Meadow Wk. EH4	6	M15
North Meggetland EH14	30	K14
North Pk. Ter. EH4	19	L17
North Peffer Pl. EH16	33	P14
North Richmond St. EH8	20	N16
West Adam St.		
North St. Andrew La. EH2	7	M17
North St. Andrew St.		
North St. Andrew St. EH2	7	M17
North St. David St. EH2	6	M17
North Wk., The EH10	31	L13
North Way, The EH8	22	P16
North Werber Pk. EH4	10	K18
North Werber Pl. EH4	10	K18
North Werber Rd. EH4	10	K18
North W. Circ. Pl. EH3	6	L17
North Wynd, Dalk. EH22	50	U10
Northcote St. EH11	19	K15
Northfield Av. EH8	22	P16
Northfield Bdy. EH8	22	P17
Northfield Circ. EH8	22	P16
Northfield Cres. EH8	22	P16
Northfield Dr. EH8	22	Q16
Northfield Fm. Av. EH8	22	Q16
Northfield Fm. Rd. EH8	22	Q16
Northfield Gdns. EH8	22	Q16
Northfield Gro. EH8	22	Q16
Northfield Pk. EH8	22	Q16
Northfield Pk. Gro. EH8	22	Q16
Northfield Rd. EH8	22	P16
Northfield Sq. EH8	22	Q16
Northfield Ter. EH8	21	P16
Willowbrae Rd.		
Northlawn Ter. EH4	9	G18
Northumberland Pl. EH3	6	M17
Northumberland St.		
Northumberland Pl. La. EH3	6	M17
Northumberland St. EH3	6	M17

Northumberland St. N. E. La. 6 M17
EH3
Northumberland St. N. W. La. 6 M17
EH3
Northumberland St. S. E. La. 6 M17
EH3
Northumberland St. S. W. La. 6 M17
EH3
Northview Ct. EH4 10 H19
Norton Pk. EH7 21 O17

Oak La. EH12 17 G17
Oakfield Pl. EH8 7 N16
Oakville Ter. EH6 13 O18
Observatory Grn. EH9 32 N13
Observatory Rd. EH9 32 N13
Ochiltree Gdns. EH16 33 P13
Ogilvie Ter. EH11 31 K14
Old Assembly Clo. EH1 7 M16
High St.
Old Broughton EH3 7 M17
Old Burdiehouse Rd. EH17 42 O10
Old Ch. La. EH15 21 P15
Old Dalkeith Rd. EH16 33 O14
Old Dalkeith Rd. EH17 33 O14
Old Dalkeith Rd. 51 R12
(Dand.), Dalk. EH22
Old Edinburgh Rd., 50 T10
Dalk. EH22
Old Fm. Av. EH13 40 H12
Old Fm. Pl. EH13 40 H12
Old Fishmarket Clo. EH1 7 M16
Old Kirk Rd. EH12 17 G16
Old Mill La. EH16 33 O13
Old Newmills Rd., Bal. EH14 45 C10
Old Quadrangle EH1 7 M16
South Bri.
Old Tolbooth Wynd EH8 7 N16
Olive Bk. Rd., Muss. EH21 24 U15
Orchard Bk. EH4 18 K17
Orchard Brae EH4 19 K17
Orchard Brae Av. EH4 19 K17
Orchard Brae Gdns. EH4 19 K17
Orchard Brae Gdns. W. EH4 18 K17
Orchard Brae W. EH4 19 K17
Orchard Brae
Orchard Cres. EH4 18 J17
Orchard Dr. EH4 18 J17
Orchard Gro. EH4 19 K17
Orchard Pl. EH4 19 K17
Orchard Rd. EH4 18 K17
Orchard Rd. S. EH4 18 J17
Orchard Ter. EH4 18 K17
Orchard Toll EH4 18 K17
Orchard Vw., Dalk. EH22 49 T9
Orchardfield Av. EH17 17 F15
Orchardfield La. EH6 12 N18
Orchardhead Ln. EH16 42 O12
Orchardhead Rd. EH16 42 O12
Ormelie Ter. EH15 23 S16
Ormidale Ter. EH12 18 J16
Ormiston Ter. EH12 17 F15
Orrok Pk. EH16 33 O13
Orwell Pl. EH11 19 K15
Orwell Ter. EH11 19 K15
Osborne Ter. EH12 19 K16
Oswald Ct. EH9 32 M14
Oswald Rd. EH9 32 M14
Oswald Ter. EH12 16 F15
Otterburn Pk. EH14 40 H12
Oxcraig St. EH5 11 K20
Oxford St. EH8 20 N15
Oxford Ter. EH4 6 L17
Oxgangs Av. EH13 40 K11
Oxgangs Bk. EH13 40 K11
Oxgangs Brae EH13 40 K11
Oxgangs Bdy. EH13 40 K11
Oxgangs Cres. EH13 40 K12
Oxgangs Dr. EH13 40 K12
Oxgangs Fm. Av. EH13 40 K11
Oxgangs Fm. Dr. EH13 40 K11
Oxgangs Fm. Gdns. EH13 40 K11
Oxgangs Fm. Gro. EH13 40 K11
Oxgangs Fm. Ln. EH13 40 K11
Oxgangs Fm. Ter. EH13 40 K11
Oxgangs Gdns. EH13 40 K12
Oxgangs Grn. EH13 40 K12
Oxgangs Gro. EH13 40 K12
Oxgangs Hill EH13 41 K12
Oxgangs Ln. EH13 40 K12
Oxgangs Medway EH13 40 K11

Oxgangs Pk. EH13 40 K11
Oxgangs Path EH13 40 K11
Oxgangs Brae
Oxgangs Path E. EH13 40 K11
Oxgangs Pl. EH13 40 K12
Oxgangs Ri. EH13 40 K12
Oxgangs Rd. EH10 40 K11
Oxgangs Rd. N. EH13 40 K11
Oxgangs Rd. N. EH14 40 J12
Oxgangs Row EH13 40 K11
Oxgangs St. EH13 40 K11
Oxgangs Ter. EH13 40 K11
Oxgangs Vw. EH13 40 K11

Paddock, The, Muss. EH21 25 V16
Balcarres Rd.
Paddockholm, The EH12 17 G15
Paisley Av. EH8 21 P16
Paisley Cres. EH8 21 P16
Paisley Dr. EH8 21 P16
Paisley Gdns. EH8 21 P16
Paisley Gro. EH8 21 P16
Paisley Ter. EH8 21 P16
Palmer Pl., Currie EH14 37 D10
Palmer Rd., Currie EH14 37 D11
Palmerston Pl. EH12 19 K16
Palmerston Pl. La. EH12 19 L16
Palmerston Pl.
Palmerston Rd. EH9 32 M15
Pankhurst Ln., Dalk. EH22 50 V10
Panmure Pl. EH3 6 M15
Pape's Cotts. EH12 18 J16
Paradykes Av., Loanh. EH20 47 O8
Park Av. EH15 22 R16
Park Av., Loanh. EH20 47 O8
Park Av., Muss. EH21 25 W15
Park Ct., Muss. EH21 25 W15
Park Cres. EH16 42 O12
Park Cres., Bonny. EH19 49 R8
Park Cres., Loanh. EH20 47 O8
Park Gdns. EH16 42 O12
Park Gdns., Muss. EH21 25 W15
Park Gro. EH16 42 O12
Park Gro. Pl., Muss. EH21 25 W15
Park Gro. Ter., Muss. EH21 25 W15
Park La., Dalk. EH22 50 T9
Park La., Muss. EH21 25 W15
Park Pl. EH6 11 M19
Park Rd., Bonny. EH19 49 R8
Park Rd., Dalk. EH22 50 T9
Park Ter. 35 T14
(Newcr.), Muss. EH21
Park Vw., Loanh. EH20 47 O8
Park Vw., Muss. EH21 25 W15
Park Vw. 35 S14
(Newcr.), Muss. EH21
Parker Av. EH7 22 Q17
Parker Rd. EH7 22 Q17
Parker Ter. EH7 22 Q17
Parkgrove Av. EH4 16 F17
Parkgrove Bk. EH4 16 F17
Parkgrove Cres. EH4 16 F17
Parkgrove Dr. EH4 16 F17
Parkgrove Gdns. EH4 16 F17
Parkgrove Grn. EH4 16 F17
Parkgrove Ln. EH4 16 F17
Parkgrove Neuk EH4 16 F17
Parkgrove Path EH4 16 F17
Parkgrove Ter.
Parkgrove Pl. EH4 16 F17
Parkgrove Rd. EH4 16 F17
Parkgrove Row EH4 16 F17
Parkgrove St. EH4 16 F17
Parkgrove Ter. EH4 16 F17
Parkgrove Vw. EH4 16 F17
Parkhead Av. EH11 29 G13
Parkhead Cres. EH11 29 G13
Parkhead Dr. EH11 29 G13
Parkhead Gdns. EH11 29 G13
Parkhead Gro. EH11 29 G13
Parkhead Ln. EH11 29 G13
Parkhead Pl. EH11 29 G13
Parkhead St. EH11 29 G13
Parkhead Ter. EH11 29 G13
Parkhead Vw. EH11 29 G13
Parkside Pl., Dalk. EH22 50 U10
Parkside St. EH8 7 N15
Parkside Ter. EH16 20 N15
Parkvale Pl. EH6 13 O18

Parliament Pl. EH6 12 N19
Parliament St.
Parliament Sq. EH1 7 M16
Parliament Sq. EH6 12 M20
Newhaven Pl.
Parliament St. EH6 12 N19
Parrotshot EH15 34 R15
Parsonage, Muss. EH21 25 V15
Parsons Grn. Ter. EH8 21 P17
Patie's Rd. EH14 40 J12
Patrick Geddes Steps EH1 20 M16
Patriothall EH3 19 L17
Hamilton Pl.
Pattison St. EH6 12 O19
Peacock Ct. EH6 12 M20
Newhaven Pl.
Peacocktail Clo. EH15 35 R14
Pearce Av. EH12 16 F16
Pearce Gro. EH12 16 F16
Pearce Rd. EH12 16 F16
Peatville Gdns. EH14 29 H13
Peatville Ter. EH14 29 H13
Peel Ter. EH9 32 N14
Peffer Bk. EH16 33 P14
Peffer Pl. EH16 33 P14
Peffer St. EH16 33 P14
Peffermill Ct. EH16 33 P14
Peffermill Rd. EH16 33 O14
Peggy's Mill Rd. EH4 8 E18
Pembroke Pl. EH12 19 K16
Pendreich Av., Bonny. EH19 49 S8
Pendreich Dr., Bonny. EH19 49 S8
Pendreich Gro., Bonny. EH19 49 S8
Pendreich Ter., Bonny. EH19 49 S8
Pendreich Vw., Bonny. EH19 49 S8
Pennywell Cotts. EH4 10 H19
Pennywell Ct. EH4 10 H19
Pennywell Gdns. EH4 9 H19
Pennywell Gro. EH4 10 H19
Pennywell Medway EH4 9 H19
Pennywell Pl. EH4 10 H19
Pennywell Rd. EH4 10 H19
Pennywell Vills. EH4 10 H19
Pentland Av. EH13 39 H11
Pentland Av., Currie EH14 37 D10
Pentland Cres. EH10 41 L12
Pentland Dr. EH10 41 K11
Pentland Gdns. EH10 41 L12
Pentland Gro. EH10 41 L12
Pentland Ind. Est., Loanh. 47 N8
EH20
Pentland Pl., Currie EH14 37 D10
Pentland Rd. EH10 46 M9
Pentland Rd. EH13 39 H12
Pentland Rd., Bonny. EH19 48 R8
Pentland Rd., Loanh. EH20 46 M9
Pentland Ter. EH10 41 L12
Pentland Vw. EH10 41 L11
Pentland Vw., Currie EH14 37 D10
Pentland Vw., Dalk. EH22 50 V9
Pentland Vw. Ct., Currie 37 D10
EH14
Pentland Vills., Jun.Grn. EH14 38 F11
Juniper Av.
Perdrixknowe EH14 30 J14
Persevere Ct. EH6 12 N19
Perth St. EH3 19 L17
Pettigrew's Clo., Dalk. EH22 50 U10
Peveril Ter. EH16 42 O12
Picardy Pl. EH1 7 M17
Pier Pl. EH6 11 M20
Piersfield Gro. EH8 21 P17
Piersfield Pl. EH8 21 P17
Piersfield Ter. EH8 21 P17
Piershill La. EH8 21 P17
Piershill Pl. EH8 21 P17
Piershill Sq. E. EH8 21 P17
Piershill Sq. W. EH8 21 P17
Piershill Ter. EH8 21 P17
Pillars, The EH17 43 P12
Pilrig Cotts. EH6 12 N18
Pilrig Gdns. EH6 12 N18
Pilrig Glebe EH6 12 N18
Pilrig Ho. Clo. EH6 12 N18
Pilrig Pl. EH6 12 N18
Pilrig St. EH6 12 N18
Pilton Av. EH5 10 K19
Pilton Cres. EH5 10 K19
Pilton Dr. EH5 10 K19
Pilton Dr. N. EH5 10 K19
Pilton Gdns. EH5 10 K19

Name		
Riverside Gdns., Muss. EH21	24	U15
Roanshead Rd.	50	V8
(Easth.), Dalk. EH22		
Robb's Ln. EH14	30	J14
Robb's Ln. Gro. EH14	30	J14
Robert Burns Dr. EH16	33	O13
Robert Burn's Ms., Dalk. EH22	50	V10
Robertson Av. EH11	30	J15
Robertson's Clo. EH1	7	N16
Robertson's Clo., Dalk. EH22	50	U10
St. Andrew St.		
Robertson's Ct. EH8	7	N16
Calton Rd.		
Rocheid Pk. EH4	10	K18
Rocheid Path EH3	11	L18
Rochester Ter. EH10	31	L14
Rockville Ter., Bonny. EH19	49	R8
Roddinglaw EH12	26	C14
Roddinglaw Rd. EH12	26	C14
Rodney St. EH7	20	M17
Romero Pl. EH16	33	N15
Ronaldson's Wf. EH6	12	N19
Sandport Pl.		
Rose Pk. EH5	11	L19
Rose St. EH2	6	L16
Rose St. N. La. EH2	6	L16
Rose St. S. La. EH2	6	L16
Rosebank Cotts. EH3	6	L16
Rosebank Gdns. EH5	11	L19
Rosebank Gro. EH5	11	L19
Rosebank Rd. EH5	11	L19
Rosebery Cres. EH12	19	K16
Rosebery Cres. La. EH12	19	K16
Roseburn Av. EH12	18	J16
Roseburn Cliff EH12	18	J16
Roseburn Cres. EH12	18	J16
Roseburn Dr. EH12	18	J16
Roseburn Gdns. EH12	18	J16
Roseburn Pl. EH12	18	J16
Roseburn St. EH12	18	J15
Roseburn Ter. EH12	18	J16
Rosefield Av. EH15	22	R16
Rosefield Av. La. EH15	22	R16
Rosefield La. EH15	22	R16
Rosefield Pl. EH15	22	R16
Rosefield St. EH15	22	R16
Rosemount Bldgs. EH3	6	L16
Roseneath Pl. EH9	20	M15
Roseneath St. EH9	20	M15
Roseneath Ter. EH9	20	M15
Rosevale Pl. EH6	13	O18
Rosevale Ter. EH6	12	O18
Roseville Gdns. EH5	11	M19
Ross Gdns. EH9	32	N14
Ross Pl. EH9	32	N14
Ross Rd. EH16	33	O13
Rossie Pl. EH7	21	O17
Rosslyn Cres. EH6	12	N18
Rosslyn Ter. EH6	12	N18
Rothesay Ms. EH3	19	K16
Rothesay Pl. EH3	19	L16
Rothesay Pl., Muss. EH21	25	V15
Rothesay Ter. EH3	19	L16
Roull Gro. EH12	29	F15
Roull Pl. EH12	29	G15
Roull Rd. EH12	29	F15
Rowallan Ct. EH12	16	E16
Craigievar Wynd		
Rowan Tree Av., Currie EH14	45	D10
Rowan Tree Gro., Currie EH14	45	D10
Roxburgh Pl. EH8	7	N16
Roxburgh St. EH8	7	N16
Roxburgh Ter. EH8	7	N16
Drummond St.		
Royal Circ. EH3	6	L17
Royal Cres. EH3	20	M17
Royal Pk. Pl. EH8	21	O17
Royal Pk. Ter. EH8	21	O17
Royal Ter. EH7	7	N17
Royal Ter. Gdns. EH7	7	N17
Royal Ter. Ms. EH7	7	N17
Royston Mains Av. EH5	10	J19
Royston Mains Clo. EH5	10	K19
Royston Mains Cres. EH5	10	J19
Royston Mains Gdns. EH5	10	K19
Royston Mains Grn. EH5	10	K19
Royston Mains Pl. EH5	10	J19
Royston Mains Rd. EH5	10	K19
Royston Mains St. EH5	10	J19
Royston Ter. EH3	11	L18
Russell Pl. EH5	11	L19
Russell Rd. EH11	18	K15
Russell Rd. EH12	18	K16
Rustic Cotts. EH14	30	J13
Colinton Rd.		
Rutherford Dr. EH16	33	O13
Rutland Ct. EH3	6	L16
Rutland Ct. La. EH3	6	L16
Rutland Pl. EH1	6	L16
West End		
Rutland Sq. EH1	6	L16
Rutland St. EH1	6	L16
Ryehill Av. EH6	13	O18
Ryehill Gdns. EH6	13	O18
Ryehill Gro. EH6	13	O18
Ryehill Pl. EH6	13	O18
Ryehill Ter. EH6	13	O18
Saddletree Ln. EH16	33	P13
St. Alban's Rd. EH9	32	M14
St. Andrew Pl. EH6	12	O18
St. Andrew Sq. EH1	7	M17
St. Andrew Sq. EH2	7	M17
St. Andrew St., Dalk. EH22	50	U10
St. Anthony Ct. EH6	12	N19
St. Anthony St.		
St. Anthony La. EH6	12	N19
St. Anthony St.		
St. Anthony Pl. EH6	12	N19
St. Anthony St. EH6	12	N19
St. Bernard's Cres. EH4	6	L17
St. Bernard's Pl. EH3	19	L17
Saunders St.		
St. Bernard's Row EH4	19	L17
St. Catherine's Gdns. EH12	17	H15
St. Catherine's Pl. EH9	32	N15
St. Clair Av. EH6	12	O18
St. Clair Pl. EH6	12	O18
St. Clair Rd. EH6	12	O18
St. Clair St. EH6	12	O18
St. Clair Ter. EH10	31	K13
St. Colme St. EH3	6	L16
St. David's Pl. EH3	6	L16
Morrison St.		
St. David's Ter. EH3	6	L16
Morrison St.		
St. Fillan's Ter. EH10	31	L13
St. Giles' St. EH1	7	M16
St. James Cen. EH1	7	M17
St. James Pl. EH1	7	M17
St. James Sq. EH1	7	M17
James Craig Wk.		
St. John St. EH8	7	N16
St. John's Av. EH12	17	G15
St. John's Cres. EH12	17	G15
St. John's Gdns. EH12	17	G15
St. John's Hill EH8	7	N16
St. John's Pl. EH8	7	N16
Holyrood Rd.		
St. John's Rd. EH12	16	F15
St. John's Ter. EH12	17	G15
St. Katharine's Brae EH16	42	O11
St. Katharine's Cres. EH16	42	O11
St. Katharine's Ln. EH16	42	O11
St. Leonard's Bk. EH8	7	N15
St. Leonard's Crag EH8	7	N15
St. Leonard's Hill EH8	7	N15
St. Leonard's La. EH8	7	N15
St. Leonard's St. EH8	20	N15
St. Margaret's Pl. EH9	32	M14
St. Margaret's Rd. EH9	31	L14
St. Mark's La. EH15	23	R16
St. Mark's Pl. EH15	23	R16
St. Mary's Pl. EH15	23	S16
St. Mary's Pl. La. EH15	23	S16
St. Mary's St. EH1	7	N16
St. Michael's Av., Muss. EH21	25	V15
St. Ninian's Dr. EH12	16	F16
St. Ninian's Rd. EH12	16	F16
St. Ninian's Ter. EH10	31	K13
St. Patrick Sq. EH8	7	N15
St. Patrick St. EH8	7	N15
St. Peter's Bldgs. EH3	19	L15
Gilmore Pl.		
St. Peter's Pl. EH3	19	L15
St. Ronan's Ter. EH10	31	L13
St. Stephen Pl. EH3	19	L17
St. Stephen St.		
St. Stephen St. EH3	6	L17
St. Teresa Pl. EH10	31	N14
St. Thomas Rd. EH9	32	M14
St. Vincent St. EH3	6	L17
Salamander Pl. EH6	12	O19
Salamander St. EH6	12	O19
Salisbury Pl. EH9	32	N15
Salisbury Rd. EH16	32	N15
Salmond Pl. EH7	21	O17
Salter's Gro., Dalk. EH22	50	V10
Salter's Rd., Dalk. EH22	50	V10
Salter's Rd., Muss. EH21	25	W13
Salter's Ter., Dalk. EH22	50	V10
Saltire Society EH1	7	M16
High St.		
Salvesen Cres. EH4	9	H19
Salvesen Gdns. EH4	9	H19
Salvesen Gro. EH4	9	H19
Salvesen Ter. EH4	9	H19
Sandford Gdns. EH15	22	R16
Sandport EH6	12	O19
Sandport Pl. EH6	12	N19
Sandport St. EH6	12	N19
Sauchiebank EH11	18	K15
Saughton Av. EH11	30	J15
Saughton Cres. EH12	18	H15
Saughton Gdns. EH12	18	H15
Saughton Gro. EH12	18	H15
Saughton Ln. EH12	18	H15
Saughton Mains Av. EH11	29	G14
Saughton Mains Bk. EH11	29	H14
Saughton Mains Cotts. EH11	29	G14
Saughton Mains Gdns.		
Saughton Mains Dr. EH11	29	G14
Saughton Mains Gdns. EH11	29	G14
Saughton Mains Gro. EH11	29	H14
Saughton Mains Ln. EH11	29	G14
Saughton Mains Pk. EH11	29	G14
Saughton Mains Pl. EH11	29	G14
Saughton Mains St. EH11	29	G14
Saughton Mains Ter. EH11	29	G14
Saughton Pk. EH12	18	H15
Saughton Rd. EH11	29	G14
Saughton Rd. N. EH12	29	G15
Saughtonhall Av. EH12	18	H15
Saughtonhall Av. W. EH12	18	H15
Saughtonhall Circ. EH12	18	J15
Saughtonhall Cres. EH12	18	H15
Saughtonhall Dr. EH12	18	H15
Saughtonhall Gdns. EH12	18	J15
Saughtonhall Gro. EH12	18	J15
Saughtonhall Pl. EH12	18	H15
Saughtonhall Ter. EH12	18	J15
Saunders St. EH3	6	L17
Savile Pl. EH9	32	N14
Savile Ter. EH9	32	N14
Saxe Coburg St. EH3	19	L17
Saxe-Coburg Pl. EH3	19	L17
Saxe-Coburg Ter. EH3	19	L17
Saxe Coburg St.		
School Brae EH4	8	E19
School Brae, Lass. EH18	48	R9
School Grn., Lass. EH18	49	R9
Sciennes EH9	32	N15
Sciennes Gdns. EH9	32	N15
Sciennes Hill Pl. EH9	32	N15
Sciennes		
Sciennes Ho. Dr. EH9	32	N15
Sciennes		
Sciennes Ho. Pl. EH9	32	N15
Sciennes Pl. EH9	32	N15
Sciennes Rd. EH9	32	M15
Scollon Av., Bonny. EH19	49	S8
Scone Gdns. EH8	21	P17
Scotland St. EH3	20	M17
Seacot EH6	13	P18
Seafield Av. EH6	13	P18
Seafield Moor Rd. EH10	46	M9
Seafield Pl. EH6	13	P18
Seafield Rd. EH6	13	P18
Seafield Rd. E. EH15	22	Q16
Seafield St. EH6	13	P18
Seafield Ter. EH6	13	P18
Seafield Av.		
Seafield Way EH15	13	Q18
Seaforth Dr. EH4	18	J17
Seaforth Ter. EH4	18	J17
Sealcarr St. EH5	10	K20
Seaport St. EH6	12	O19
Bernard St.		
Seaview Cres. EH15	23	S16
Seaview Ter. EH15	23	S16
Second Gait	37	D12
(Ricc.), Currie EH14		
Semple St. EH3	6	L16

Street	Map	Grid
Seton Pl. EH9	32	N15
Shadepark Cres., Dalk. EH22	50	U10
Shadepark Dr., Dalk. EH22	50	U10
Shadepark Gdns., Dalk. EH22	50	U10
Shaftesbury Pk. EH11	30	K14
Shandon Cres. EH11	30	K14
Shandon Pl. EH11	30	K14
Shandon Rd. EH11	30	K14
Shandon St. EH11	30	K14
Shandon Ter. EH11	30	K14
Shandwick Pl. EH2	6	L16
Shanter Way EH16	33	O13
Cumnor Cres.		
Sharpdale Ln. EH16	33	O13
Shaw's Pl. EH7	12	N18
Shaw's Sq. EH1	20	N17
Gayfield Sq.		
Shaw's St. EH7	12	N18
Shaw's Ter. EH7	12	N18
Sheriff Bk. EH6	12	N19
Sheriff Brae EH6	12	N19
Sheriff Pk. EH6	12	N19
Shore EH6	12	O19
Shore Pl. EH6	12	O19
Shorthope St., Muss. EH21	25	V15
Shrub Mt. EH15	22	R17
Shrub Pl. EH7	12	N18
Shrub Pl. La. EH7	20	N17
Shrub Pl.		
Sienna Gdns. EH9	32	N15
Sighthill Av. EH11	29	G13
Sighthill Bk. EH11	28	F13
Sighthill Ct. EH11	28	F13
Sighthill Cres. EH11	28	F13
Sighthill Dr. EH11	28	F13
Sighthill Gdns. EH11	29	F13
Sighthill Grn. EH11	28	F13
Sighthill Gro. EH11	29	G13
Sighthill Ln. EH11	28	F13
Sighthill Neuk EH11	28	F13
Sighthill Pk. EH11	29	F13
Sighthill Pl. EH11	28	F13
Sighthill Ri. EH11	28	F13
Sighthill Rd. EH11	28	F13
Sighthill St. EH11	28	F13
Sighthill Ter. EH11	29	F13
Sighthill Vw. EH11	28	F13
Sighthill Wynd EH11	28	F13
Silverknowes Av. EH4	9	G18
Silverknowes Bk. EH4	9	G18
Silverknowes Brae EH4	9	G18
Silverknowes Ct. EH4	9	G18
Silverknowes Cres. EH4	9	G18
Silverknowes Dell EH4	9	G18
Silverknowes Dr. EH4	9	G18
Silverknowes Eastway EH4	9	G18
Silverknowes Gdns. EH4	9	G19
Silverknowes Grn. EH4	9	H18
Silverknowes Gro. EH4	9	G18
Silverknowes Hill EH4	9	G18
Silverknowes Ln. EH4	9	G18
Silverknowes Midway EH4	9	H18
Silverknowes Neuk EH4	9	H18
Silverknowes Parkway EH4	9	G19
Silverknowes Pl. EH4	9	G18
Silverknowes Rd. EH4	9	G19
Silverknowes Rd. E. EH4	9	G18
Silverknowes Rd. S. EH4	9	G18
Silverknowes Southway EH4	9	H18
Silverknowes Ter. EH4	9	G18
Silverknowes Vw. EH4	9	H18
Silvermills EH3	19	L17
Simon Sq. EH8	7	N16
Sir Harry Lauder Rd. EH15	22	R16
Slaeside, Bal. EH14	45	C9
Slateford Rd. EH11	30	J14
Slateford Rd. EH14	30	J14
Sleigh Dr. EH7	21	O17
Sleigh Gdns. EH7	21	P17
Sloan St. EH6	12	N18
Smeaton Gro.	25	V14
(Inver.), Muss. EH21		
Smithfield St. EH11	30	J15
Smith's Pl. EH6	12	N18
Smithy Grn. Av.	51	R12
(Dand.), Dalk. EH22		
Society EH1	7	M16
Chambers St.		
Solicitor's Bldgs. EH1	7	M16
Cowgate		
Somerset Pl. EH6	12	O18

Street	Map	Grid
Sour Howe EH13	40	K11
South Barnton Av. EH4	9	G18
South Beechwood EH12	17	H15
South Bri. EH1	7	M16
South Bri. EH8	7	M16
South Charlotte St. EH2	6	L16
South Clerk St. EH8	20	N15
South Coll. St. EH8	7	M16
South E. Circ. Pl. EH3	6	L17
South Elixa Pl. EH8	22	P16
South Ettrick Rd. EH10	31	K14
South Fort St. EH6	12	N19
South Gayfield La. EH1	20	N17
Gayfield Sq.		
South Gillsland Rd. EH10	31	K14
South Gray St. EH9	32	N14
South Gray's Clo. EH1	7	N16
South Groathill Av. EH4	18	J17
South Gyle Access EH12	28	F14
South Gyle Bdy. EH12	27	D15
South Gyle Cres. EH12	28	E14
South Gyle Cres. La. EH12	28	E14
South Gyle Gdns. EH12	28	E15
South Gyle Ln. EH12	28	E15
South Gyle Mains EH12	28	E15
South Gyle Pk. EH12	28	E15
South Gyle Rd. EH12	28	E15
South Gyle Wynd EH12	28	F14
South Lauder Rd. EH9	32	N14
South Laverockbank Av. EH5	11	M19
South Learmonth Av. EH4	19	K17
South Learmonth Gdns. EH4	19	K17
South Lorne Pl. EH6	12	N18
South Maybury EH12	16	E15
South Meadow Wk. EH9	32	M15
Roseneath Ter.		
South Mellis Pk. EH8	22	Q16
South Morton St. EH15	23	S16
South Oswald Rd. EH9	32	M14
South Oxford St. EH8	32	N15
South Pk. EH6	11	M19
South St. Andrew St. EH2	7	M17
South St. David St. EH2	7	M17
South Sloan St. EH6	12	N18
South St., Dalk. EH22	50	U10
South St., Muss. EH21	24	U15
South Trinity Rd. EH5	11	L19
Southfield Bk. EH15	22	Q15
Southfield Fm. Gro. EH15	22	Q16
Southfield Gdns. E. EH15	22	Q16
Southfield Gdns. W. EH15	22	Q16
Southfield Ln. EH15	22	Q15
Southfield Pl. EH15	22	R16
Southfield Pl. N. EH15	22	Q15
Southfield Sq.		
Southfield Pl. S. EH15	22	Q15
Southfield Sq.		
Southfield Rd. E. EH15	22	Q15
Southfield Rd. W. EH15	22	Q15
Southfield Sq. EH15	22	Q15
Southfield Ter. EH15	22	Q15
Southfield Vills. EH15	22	R16
Stanley St.		
Southhouse Av. EH17	42	O11
Southhouse Bdy. EH17	42	O10
Southhouse Cres. EH17	43	O10
Southhouse Gdns. EH17	42	O10
Southhouse Gro. EH17	42	O10
Southhouse Ln. EH17	42	O11
Southhouse Medway EH17	43	O11
Southhouse Path EH17	43	O11
Southhouse Rd. EH17	42	O11
Southhouse Sq. EH17	43	O10
Southhouse Ter. EH17	43	P11
Soutra Ct. EH16	43	O11
Spa Pl. EH15	22	R17
Spalding Cres., Dalk. EH22	50	U10
Speedwell Av., Dalk. EH22	51	R12
Spence St. EH16	33	N15
Spencer Pl. EH5	11	L19
Spey St. EH7	12	N18
Spey St. La. EH7	12	N18
Spey Ter. EH7	12	N18
Spiers Pl. EH6	12	N19
Spinney, The EH17	43	P11
Spittal St. EH3	6	L16
Spittal St. La. EH3	6	L16
Spittalfield Cres. EH8	20	N15
St. Leonard's St.		
Spottiswoode Rd. EH9	32	M15

Street	Map	Grid
Spottiswoode St. EH9	32	M15
Spring Gdns. EH8	21	O17
Springfield EH6	12	N18
Springfield Bldgs. EH6	12	N18
Springfield St.		
Springfield La. EH6	12	N18
Springfield St. EH6	12	N18
Springvalley Gdns. EH10	31	L14
Springvalley Ter. EH10	31	L14
Springwell Pl. EH11	19	K15
Springwood Pk. EH16	42	O12
Spylaw Av. EH13	39	G12
Spylaw Bk. Rd. EH13	39	G12
Spylaw Ho. EH13	39	H11
Spylaw Pk. EH13	39	G12
Spylaw Rd. EH10	31	K14
Spylaw St. EH13	39	H11
Square, The	51	R12
(Dand.), Dalk. EH22		
Stable La. EH10	31	L14
Stafford St. EH3	6	L16
Stair Pk. EH12	18	J16
Stanedykehead EH16	42	N11
Stanhope Pl. EH12	19	K16
Stanhope St. EH12	19	K16
Stanley Pl. EH7	21	O17
Stanley Rd. EH6	11	M19
Stanley St. EH15	22	R16
Stanwell St. EH6	12	N18
Stapeley Av. EH7	22	Q17
Starbank Rd. EH5	11	M19
Station Brae EH15	22	R16
Station Ln., Bal. EH14	45	C10
Station Rd. EH12	17	G15
Station Rd., Dalk. EH22	50	T9
Station Rd., Loanh. EH20	48	P8
Station Rd., Muss. EH21	24	U15
Stead's Pl. EH6	12	N18
Steel's Pl. EH10	31	L14
Steils, The EH10	40	K12
Stenhouse Av. EH11	29	H14
Stenhouse Av. W. EH11	29	H14
Stenhouse Cotts. EH11	29	H14
Stenhouse Cres. EH11	29	H14
Stenhouse Cross EH11	29	H14
Stenhouse Dr. EH11	29	H14
Stenhouse Gdns. EH11	29	H14
Stenhouse Gdns. N. EH11	29	H14
Stenhouse Gro. EH11	29	H14
Stenhouse Mill Cres. EH11	29	H14
Stenhouse Mill La. EH11	29	H14
Stenhouse Mill Wynd EH11	29	H14
Stenhouse Pl. E. EH11	29	H14
Stenhouse Pl. W. EH11	29	H14
Stenhouse Rd. EH11	29	H14
Stenhouse St. E. EH11	29	H14
Stenhouse St. W. EH11	29	G14
Stenhouse Ter. EH11	29	H14
Stennis Gdns. EH17	43	P12
Stevenlaw's Clo. EH1	7	M16
High St.		
Stevenson Av. EH11	30	J15
Stevenson Dr. EH11	29	H14
Stevenson Gro. EH11	30	J15
Stevenson Rd. EH11	30	J15
Stevenson Ter. EH11	30	J15
Stewart Av., Currie EH14	37	D10
Stewart Cres., Currie EH14	37	D10
Stewart Gdns., Currie EH14	37	D10
Stewart Gro., Dalk. EH22	51	R12
Stewart Pl., Currie EH14	37	D10
Stewart Rd., Currie EH14	37	D10
Stewart Ter. EH11	30	J15
Stewartfield EH6	12	M18
Stirling Rd. EH5	11	L19
Stoneybank Av., Muss. EH21	24	U14
Stoneybank Ct., Muss. EH21	24	U15
Stoneybank Cres., Muss. EH21	24	U14
Stoneybank Dr., Muss. EH21	24	U15
Stoneybank Gdns.,	24	U15
Muss. EH21		
Stoneybank Gdns. N.,	24	U15
Muss. EH21		
Stoneybank Gdns. S.,	24	U14
Muss. EH21		
Stoneybank Gro.,	24	U14
Muss. EH21		
Stoneybank Pl., Muss. EH21	24	U14
Stoneybank Rd., Muss. EH21	24	U14
Stoneybank Ter., Muss. EH21	24	U14
Stoneyhill Av., Muss. EH21	24	U15

Street	Map	Ref
Wardie Rd. EH5	11	L19
Wardie Sq. EH5	11	L19
Wardie Steps EH5	11	L19
Wardieburn Dr. EH5	11	K19
Wardieburn Pl. E. EH5	10	K19
Wardieburn Pl. N. EH5	10	K19
Wardieburn Pl. S. EH5	10	K19
Wardieburn Pl. W. EH5	10	K19
Wardieburn Rd. EH5	10	K19
Wardieburn St. E. EH5	10	K19
Wardieburn St. W. EH5	10	K19
Wardieburn Ter. EH5	10	K19
Wardiefield EH5	11	K19
Wardlaw Pl. EH11	30	K15
Wardlaw St. EH11	30	K15
Wardlaw Ter. EH11	30	K15
Warrender Pk. Cres. EH9	31	L15
Warrender Pk. Rd. EH9	32	M15
Warrender Pk. Ter. EH9	32	M15
Warriston Av. EH3	11	M18
Warriston Clo. EH1	7	M16
High St.		
Warriston Cres. EH3	11	M18
Warriston Dr. EH3	11	L18
Warriston Gdns. EH3	11	L18
Warriston Pl. EH3	11	M18
Warriston Rd. EH3	11	M19
Warriston Rd. EH7	11	M19
Warriston Ter. EH3	11	L18
Washington La. EH11	19	K15
Washington St. EH11	19	K15
Water St. EH6	12	O19
Waterfall Wk., Dalk. EH22	50	U9
Bruce Gdns.		
Waterloo Pl. EH1	7	M17
Water's Clo. EH6	12	O19
Shore		
Waterside Ct. EH12	18	J16
Coltbridge Av.		
Watertoun Rd. EH9	32	N14
Watson Cres. EH11	31	K15
Watson's Bldgs. EH4	9	G18
Main St.		
Watts Clo., Muss. EH21	24	U15
Wauchope Av. EH16	34	Q14
Wauchope Cres. EH16	34	Q14
Wauchope Ho. EH16	34	Q14
Wauchope Pl. EH16	34	Q14
Wauchope Rd. EH16	34	Q14
Wauchope Sq. EH16	34	Q14
Wauchope Ter. EH16	34	Q14
Waugh Path, Bonny. EH19	49	S8
Waulkmill Ln., Currie EH14	45	D10
Waverley Bri. EH1	7	M16
Waverley Ct., Bonny. EH19	49	S8
Waverley Cres., Bonny. EH19	49	S8
Waverley Dr., Bonny. EH19	49	S8
Waverley Pk. EH8	21	O17
Waverley Pk., Bonny. EH19	49	S8
Waverley Pk. Ter. EH8	21	O17
Waverley Pl. EH7	21	O17
Waverley Rd., Bonny. EH19	49	S8
Waverley Rd., Dalk. EH22	50	T9
Waverley Steps EH2	7	M16
Waverley Ter., Bonny. EH19	49	S8
Weaver's Knowe Cres.,	37	D11
Currie EH14		
Websters Land EH1	6	M16
West Port		
Wedderburn Ter.	25	V14
(Inver.), Muss. EH21		
Wee Brae, Lass. EH18	49	R9
Weir Ct. EH11	29	F13
Weir Cres., Dalk. EH22	50	T9
Well Ct. EH4	19	L16
Wellington Pl. EH6	12	O19
Wellington St. EH7	7	N17
Wemyss Pl. EH3	6	L17
Wemyss Pl. Ms. EH3	6	L17
West Adam St. EH8	7	N16
West Annandale St. EH7	12	M18
West App. Rd. EH3	6	L15
West App. Rd. EH3	6	L15
West Bow EH1	6	M16
West Bowling Grn. St. EH6	12	N19
West Brighton Cres. EH15	22	R16
West Bryson Rd. EH11	31	K15
West Caiystane Rd. EH10	41	L11
West Carnethy Av. EH13	39	H11
West Castle Rd. EH10	31	L15
West Catherine Pl. EH12	18	K16
West Coates EH12	18	K16
West Coll. St. EH8	7	M16
West Ct. EH4	18	J17
West Ct. EH16	34	Q14
West Craigs Av. EH12	15	D15
West Craigs Cres. EH12	15	D15
West Craigs Ind. Est. EH12	15	D16
West Cft.	26	A13
(Ratho), Newbr. EH28		
West Cromwell St. EH6	12	N19
Cromwell Pl.		
West Crosscauseway EH8	7	N15
West End EH2	6	L16
West End Pl. EH11	19	K15
West Ferryfield EH5	11	K18
West Fountain Pl. EH11	19	K15
West Gorgie Parks EH14	30	J14
West Gra. Gdns. EH9	32	M14
Grange Ln.		
West Granton Grn. EH4	10	H19
West Granton Gro. EH4	10	J19
West Granton Rd. EH5	10	J19
West Harbour Rd. EH5	10	K20
West Holmes Gdns.,	24	U15
Muss. EH21		
West Mains Rd. EH9	32	N13
West Maitland St. EH12	19	L16
West Mayfield EH9	32	N14
West Mill Ct., Lass. EH18	49	R8
Westmill Rd.		
West Mill La. EH4	19	K17
Dean Path		
West Mill Rd. EH13	39	G11
West Montgomery Pl. EH7	20	N17
West Newington Pl. EH9	32	N15
West Nicolson St. EH8	7	N16
West Norton Pl. EH7	20	N17
West Pk. Pl. EH11	19	K15
West Pier EH5	10	K20
West Pilton Av. EH4	10	J18
West Pilton Bk. EH4	10	H19
West Pilton Cres. EH4	10	H19
West Pilton Crossway EH4	10	J19
West Pilton Dr. EH4	10	J19
West Pilton Gdns. EH4	10	J19
West Pilton Grn. EH4	10	J19
West Pilton Gro. EH4	10	J19
West Pilton Lea EH4	10	J19
West Pilton Ln. EH4	10	J19
West Pilton March EH4	10	J19
West Pilton Pk. EH4	10	J19
West Pilton Pl. EH4	10	J19
West Pilton Ri. EH4	10	J19
West Pilton Rd. EH4	10	J19
West Pilton St. EH4	10	J19
West Pilton Ter. EH4	10	J19
West Pilton Vw. EH4	10	J18
West Port EH1	6	M16
West Port EH3	6	M16
West Powburn FH9	32	N14
West Preston St. EH8	32	N15
West Register St. EH2	7	M17
West Relugas Rd. EH9	32	M14
West Richmond St. EH8	7	N16
West Savile Rd. EH16	32	N14
West Savile Ter. EH9	32	N14
West Scotland St. La. EH3	20	M17
West Shore Rd. EH5	10	H19
West Silvermills La. EH3	19	L17
West Stanhope Pl. EH12	19	K16
Stanhope Pl.		
West Telferton EH7	22	Q17
West Tollcross EH3	6	L15
West Werberside EH4	10	K18
West Winnelstrae EH5	10	K18
West Wds. EH4	10	K18
Westbank Ln. EH15	22	R17
Westbank Pl. EH15	22	R17
Westbank St. EH15	22	R17
Westburn Av. EH14	38	F12
Westburn Gdns. EH14	38	F12
Westburn Gro. EH14	38	F12
Westburn Middlefield EH14	38	F12
Westburn Pk. EH14	38	F12
Wester Broom Av. EH12	28	F15
Wester Broom Dr. EH12	28	F15
Wester Broom Gdns. EH12	28	F15
Wester Broom Gro. EH12	28	F15
Wester Broom Pl. EH12	28	F15
Wester Broom Ter. EH12	28	F15
Wester Clo. EH6	11	M20
Newhaven Main St.		
Wester Coates Av. EH12	18	K16
Wester Coates Gdns. EH12	18	K16
Wester Coates Pl. EH12	19	K16
Wester Coates Rd. EH12	18	K16
Wester Coates Ter. EH12	18	K16
Wester Drylaw Av. EH4	10	H18
Wester Drylaw Dr. EH4	10	H18
Wester Drylaw Pk. EH4	10	J18
Wester Drylaw Pl. EH4	10	H18
Wester Drylaw Row EH4	18	J17
Wester Hailes Cen. EH14	38	F12
Wester Hailes Dr. EH14	38	F12
Wester Hailes Pk. EH14	39	G12
Wester Hailes Rd. EH11	28	F13
Wester Hailes Rd. EH14	28	F13
Wester Hailes Rd.,	28	F13
Jun.Grn. EH14		
Wester Hill EH10	40	K12
Wester Row, Currie EH14	27	D13
Wester Steil EH10	30	K13
Western Cor. EH12	18	H16
Saughtonhall Dr.		
Western Gdns. EH12	18	J16
Western Harbour EH6	12	N20
Western Pl. EH12	18	J16
Western Ter. EH12	18	J16
Westfield Av. EH11	30	J15
Westfield Ct. EH11	30	J15
Westfield Ct., Dalk. EH22	50	T9
Westfield Dr., Dalk. EH22	50	T9
Westfield Gro., Dalk. EH22	50	T9
Westfield Pk., Dalk. EH22	50	T9
Westfield Rd. EH11	30	J15
Westfield St. EH11	30	J15
Westgarth Av. EH13	39	H11
Westhall Gdns. EH10	31	L15
Westland Cotts. EH17	43	Q11
Ravenscroft Pl.		
Westland Hos. EH17	43	Q11
Ravenscroft Pl.		
Westmill Rd., Lass. EH18	49	R8
Westmill Wynd, Lass. EH18	49	R8
Westmost Clo. EH6	11	M20
Newhaven Main St.		
Westside Plaza EH14	38	F12
Murrayburn Gate		
Wheatfield Gro., Loanh. EH20	47	O8
Wheatfield Ln., Loanh. EH20	47	O9
Wheatfield Pl. EH11	30	J15
Wheatfield Rd. EH11	30	J15
Wheatfield St. EH11	30	K15
Wheatfield Ter. EH11	30	J15
Wheatfield Wk., Loanh. EH20	47	O8
Wheatsheaf La., Dalk. EH22	50	U10
Whins Pl. EH15	22	R17
Figgate St.		
White Dales EH10	41	M11
White Hart St., Dalk. EH22	50	U10
Buccleuch St.		
White Horse Clo. EH8	7	N16
White Pk. EH11	30	K15
Whitehall Ct. EH4	18	H17
Whitehill Av., Muss. EH21	24	U15
Whitehill Dr., Dalk. EH22	50	V9
Whitehill Fm. Rd.,	24	U14
Muss. EH21		
Whitehill Gdns., Muss. EH21	24	U14
Whitehill Gro., Dalk. EH22	50	V9
Whitehill Rd. EH15	35	S14
Whitehill Rd., Dalk. EH22	35	S14
Whitehill Rd.	35	S14
(Newcr.), Muss. EH21		
Whitehill St.	35	S14
(Newcr.), Muss. EH21		
Whitehouse Ln. EH9	31	L15
Whitehouse Rd. EH4	8	E18
Whitehouse Ter. EH9	32	M14
Whitelea Cres., Bal. EH14	44	C8
Whitelea Rd., Bal. EH14	44	B8
Whites Clo., Dalk. EH22	50	U10
St. Andrew St.		
Whitingford EH6	12	M19
Whitson Cres. EH11	30	H15
Whitson Gro. EH11	30	H15
Whitson Pl. E. EH11	30	H15
Whitson Pl. W. EH11	30	H15
Whitson Rd. EH11	30	H15
Whitson Ter. EH11	30	H15
Whitson Wk. EH11	30	H15

INDEX TO PLACES OF INTEREST